SHILOH

A Narrative Play

by

HOWARD
RUBENSTEIN

Granite Hills Press™

SHILOH
A Narrative Play
by Howard Rubenstein

Published 2015 by Granite Hills Press™
SAN 298-072X

Cover by Howard Rubenstein—Front: After a drawing of the Battle of Shiloh by William H. Rau, late 19th century;
Back: Map of Key Places of the Battle of Shiloh by Howard Rubenstein.

Cataloging in Publication
    Rubenstein, Howard S 1931–
        Shiloh : a narrative play / by Howard Rubenstein
            p.   cm
            LCCN: 2014913260
            ISBN-10: 1-929468-30-X
            ISBN-13: 978-1-929468-30-0
Printed in the United States of America.

PLAYS
BY HOWARD RUBENSTEIN

Agamemnon
Aeschylus' play translated with reconstructed stage directions
ISBN 978-1-929468-07-2

Britannicus
Jean Racine's play translated and adapted
ISBN 978-1-929468-14-0

Brothers All
based on Dostoyevski's novel "The Brothers Karamazov"
ISBN 978-1-929468-11-9

The Golem, Man of Earth
ISBN 978-1-929468-12-6

Romance of the Western Chamber—A Musical
co-authored with Max Lee
based on the 13th century Chinese play *Xi Xiang Ji*
ISBN 978-1-929468-28-7

Shiloh
ISBN978-1-929468-30-0

Tony and Cleo
ISBN 978-1-929468-13-3

The Trojan Women
Euripides' play translated and adapted
ISBN 978-1-929468-05-8

Dedicated

to the memory of

Brigadier General Benjamin Mayberry Prentiss,

the only Union general of three

who did not desert the Hornets' Nest,

and to the valiant men under his command

CONTENTS

PREFACE

SHILOH is a narrative play based on important events in the battle of Shiloh, a turning point in the U.S. Civil War. By a narrative play, I mean a play meant to be read and not acted on the stage. The reading, therefore, is not a phase in the development of a stage production; nor is it the reading of a play that has already been produced on the stage. The reading of a narrative play *is* the production.

The historical sources for *SHILOH* were the following:

Cunningham, O. Edward, Joiner, Gary D., and Timothy B. Smith, edits. *Shiloh and the Western Campaign of 1862*. New York: Savas Beatie, 2007.

Daniel, Larry J. *Shiloh—The Battle That Changed the Civil War*. New York: Simon & Schuster, 1997.

Logsdon, David R, compiler and editor. *Eyewitnesses at the Battle of Shiloh*. Nashville: Kettle Mills Press, 1994.

McDonough, James Lee. *Shiloh–in Hell before Night.* Knoxville: University of Tennessee Press, 1977.

McPherson, James. *Battle Cry of Freedom: The Civil War Era*. Oxford, New York: Oxford University Press, 1988.

Reed, David W. *The Battle of Shiloh and the Organizations Engaged.* Knoxville: University of Tennessee Press, 2008 (previously printed by the Government Printing Office, Washington, DC, 1903, 1909).

Sword, Wiley. *Shiloh: Bloody April.* Dayton: Morningside, 1974, 1983.

SHILOH is presented largely from the soldier's point of view. Many ordinary soldiers were literate; they wrote letters, kept journals, and otherwise wrote eyewitness accounts which, unlike many of the memoirs or reports of their commanding officers, were not embellished or glorified or otherwise distorted by attempts to justify the commanders' decisions.

The play incorporates many of the songs of the period, some of which are alluded to in the sources. The songs in the play are listed below in the order in which they appear:

PART ONE

"Cheer, Boys, Cheer!" (Anonymous, c. 1861).

"The Girl I Left Behind Me" (Anonymous, <1812).

"The Bonnie Blue Flag" (Music anonymous, Words Harry Macarthy (McCarthy), 1861).

"Say, Brother, Will You Meet Us?" (Anonymous, Camp Meeting Song, 1858).

"Lorena" (Music J. P. Webster, Words H. D. L. Webster, 1857).

"Wait for the Wagon" (Music Wiesenthal [first name lost],
    Words anonymous, 1850).

PART TWO

"Dixie" (Music Daniel D. Emmett, 1859, multiple lyrics by
    multiple lyricists, c. 1861).

"The Star Spangled Banner" (Music J. S. Smith, c. 1775,
    Words F. S. Key, 1814).

"Brave Boys Are They" (H. C. Work, 1861).

"Little Major" (H. C. Work, 1862).

"John Brown's Body" (Anonymous, Music 1858,
    Words, 1861).

"Aura Lea" (G. R. Poulton & W. W. Fosdick, 1861).

"O Hard Tack, Come Again No More" (Anonymous,1861).

"The Anvil Chorus" from the opera *Il Trovatore* (Giuseppe
    Verdi, 1853).

"Weeping, Sad and Lonely (When This Cruel War Is
    Over)" (C. C. Sawyer & H. Tucker, 1862).

"The Vacant Chair" (H. S. Washburn & G. F. Root, 1861).

"The Minstrel Boy" (Music Traditional, Words Thomas
    Moore, <1852).

"The Battle Hymn of the Republic" (Music anonymous, 1858, Words J. W. Howe, 1861).

It is curious that Civil War historians use several terms that were coined after the battle of Shiloh as if they were actually used during the battle. Probably the most famous example is the historians' term "Sunken Road," which describes an abandoned road that unexpectedly figures prominently in the battle of the Hornets' Nest. Not a single eyewitness used the term Sunken Road, but rather various descriptive terms that describe an old road that was worn down through usage and erosion. Moreover, the word "sunken" (cf. "sink hole") implies that a geological event caused the road to suddenly sink; there is no evidence that such an event occurred.

Equally curious, Civil War historians frequently refer to the Confederate General Pierre Beauregard as "the Creole." Beauregard was indeed a Creole, and it may be informative to tell the readers that once; but what is served by repeatedly using a term that describes ancestral origins rather than using his proper name? If the historians are implying that ancestral origins affect military ability, they should tell us why they believe so. It is hard to imagine a modern historian referring even once to President Obama as "the mulatto." Moreover, all the eyewitnesses at the battle of Shiloh call Beauregard only by his name.

Perhaps the greatest faux pas of the historians is to assert without citation that the name *Shiloh* is the Hebrew word for *place of peace* or *peace*. Shiloh is the name of the place where God's tabernacle first came to rest, and the etymology of the name is unknown. The word for *peace* in Hebrew is *Shalom*, a word with no more relationship to *Shiloh* than to the skiers' term *slalom*.

The premiere of *SHILOH* took place on January 17, 2015 (Part One), and January 24 (Part Two), at Pacific Regent La Jolla, San Diego, with the following cast and crew:

Commentator, Irving Tragen; Confederates, Tom Johnsrud, Elissa Pinson, Arthur Stromberg; Federals, Vic Archer, Isabelle Friedlieb, Elissa Pinson, Judy Rubenstein. Sound Engineer and Technical Advisor, Tracy Atherton; Casting Director Tom Ryan; Pacific Regent La Jolla Supervisor, Marianne Velasco.

It is a pleasure to thank the members of the cast for helping me revise the play. My deepest gratitude, however, goes to my wife, Judy, for being my principal editor.

Howard Rubenstein
San Diego
March 11, 2015

SHILOH

CHARACTERS

COMMENTATOR, the only fictional character in the play. He is an honest reporter and a true historian, an analytic interpreter of men and events, who draws conclusions based on evidence. He focuses on the important and does not try to impress by citing a myriad of facts.

CONFEDERATE SOLDIERS (also known as REBELS, GREYS, BUTTERNUTS, SECESHES)

UNION SOLDIERS (also known as FEDERALS, BLUE COATS, YANKEES)

OTHER CHARACTERS with minor roles:
>CONFEDERATE OFFICERS
>UNION OFFICERS
>DOCTOR
>SURGEON
>VOLUNTEER NURSE
>*et al.*

CONFEDERATE MILITARY BAND

CONFEDERATE CHORUS

UNION MILITARY BAND

UNION CHORUS

TIME
Early April, 1862, but especially the two days Sunday,
April 6, and Monday, April 7.

PLACE
Southwestern Tennessee and Northeastern Mississippi,
between Savannah, Tennessee, and Corinth, Mississippi,
but especially the Tennessee battlefields surrounding
Shiloh Church, Pittsburg Landing, and the "Hornets'
Nest." (see map back cover).

SET
The set is simple. The Confederate soldiers wearing gray
caps are sitting stage right, the Union soldiers wearing
blue caps stage left. There is a Confederate flag above
and behind the Confederate Soldiers, and a Union flag of
1862 above and behind the Union Soldiers.

PROLOGUE

COMMENTATOR.

The American Civil War was fought in two theaters, one in the East; and one in what was then called the West, which was bounded on the west by the Mississippi River. The Battle of Shiloh was fought in the Western theater. The South believed that if it was to continue to control the Mississippi Valley from the state of Tennessee to the Gulf of Mexico, it was essential to win the battle of Shiloh.

The play *SHILOH* tells of the battle of Shiloh, which was the first great battle in the Civil War, and also the first to show a failure of military leadership, which led to extraordinary gore and carnage and cowardice. The play and its dialogue are based on historical accounts and on original eyewitness documents–soldiers' letters, diaries, and notebooks.

The North's commanders were General Ulysses S. Grant and General Don Carlos Buell; the South's commanders were General Albert Sidney Johnston and General Pierre Beauregard. The battle lasted only two days, but the carnage was the greatest known in any American battle until that time. It was a turning point in the Civil War, for until Shiloh, both North and South thought the War would be over in a matter of a few short months; but after Shiloh, both sides realized that the War would go on for many months or even years.

On the first day of the battle, Sunday, April 6, 1862, the South was nearly victorious under the command of General Albert

Sidney Johnston.   However, General Johnston was killed during mid-afternoon of that day; and the new Confederate commander, General Pierre Beauregard, called off the battle when the Confederates were on the verge of victory, because he thought his troops needed nourishment and a good night's sleep.   That was a fatal decision.   By early morning of the second day, Monday, April 7, 1862, the North had acquired thousands of fresh troops under the leadership of General Buell; and late that morning, the North emerged from the battle of Shiloh victorious.

Be aware of two sources of possible confusion.   First, the famous song "Dixie" in the late antebellum period and very early in the Civil War, was a northern minstrel song making fun of the South.   And at the battle of Shiloh, the Union military band gave a spirited performance of it.   But very soon, "Dixie" became what we now know it as, the greatest anthem of the South.

The second source of possible confusion is that at Shiloh, the Union had two generals named Wallace.   One was Will Wallace, who, as he was deserting the Hornets' Nest, was mortally wounded.   The other was Lew Wallace, who, for unclear reasons took a circuitous route through the woods and arrived at the battle when it was nearly over.   As a result of his late arrival, Lew Wallace was militarily disgraced, but he later became famous in literary circles as the author of the great American biblical novel "Ben Hur."

But I have said enough and the show is about to begin.

CONFEDERATE MILITARY BAND.
(*Playing the* "Overture," *a spirited version of*
"Cheer, Boys, Cheer!").

PART ONE

CORINTH, MISSISSIPPI
April 1, 1862

CONFEDERATE OFFICER.
Things aren't looking good.
We Confederates have lost Kentucky and Tennessee.
Now we've got to resist the advance of the Federals
to the Gulf of Mexico.
So all our Western troops
are concentrated at Corinth, Mississippi,
the gateway to the Gulf,
with orders to defend the city.

Corinth is the junction of the main railroads
in the Mississippi Valley—the Mobile and Ohio,
running north-south,
and the Memphis and Charleston,
running east-west.
Railroads designed for carrying passengers
are now transporting troops.

Still, we Confederates are confused.
Are we to wait here and defend Corinth,
or march and attack the Yankees at Pittsburg Landing,
just twenty-three miles north in Tennessee?

According to our intelligence,
the Union commander Ulysses S. Grant
has put his army

in a very vulnerable position at Pittsburg Landing
without any artificial protection—
no breastworks, no earthworks, no trenches.
They simply are inviting an attack.

COMMENTATOR.
Steamboats deliver Federal regiments
to Pittsburg Landing every day.
General Ulysses S. Grant
commander of the Army of the Tennessee,
is planning to march on Corinth
once General Buell, commander of the Army of the Ohio,
arrives to reinforce him.

Grant spends the day at the Landing,
but returns to the comforts of the Cherry mansion
in Savannah, Tennessee, by evening.

CONFEDERATE SOLDIER.
Our confusion is over.
Our orders are to attack Pittsburg Landing
before Buell arrives,
and take Grant by surprise.

COMMENTATOR.
That soldier has a clear understanding
of his side's objectives.
That's highly unusual.
When the typical soldier left for war—
home town cheering,
bands playing, people waving,
little boys watching with admiration—
he only knew he was "fighting for country."
Is there anything more glorious than that?

CONFEDERATE MILITARY BAND (*Playing*)
and CONFEDERATE CHORUS (*Singing*
"Cheer, Boys, Cheer!").

> Cheer, boys, cheer! We'll march away to battle!
> Cheer, boys, cheer! for our sweethearts and our wives!
> Cheer, boys, cheer! We'll nobly do our duty,
> and give to the South our hearts, our arms, our lives.

COMMENTATOR.
On April 3, from Corinth,
General Albert Sidney Johnston,
the South's Commander of the Western Theater
and Commander of the Army of the Mississippi,
wrote to Jefferson Davis,
President of the Confederate States of America,
in Richmond:

"Buell is in motion to join Grant at Savannah.
I am hoping for an engagement with Grant
before Buell joins him."

By mid-afternoon on April 3,
Confederate troops began moving out of Corinth,
as regimental bands were playing
"The Girl I Left Behind Me."

CONFEDERATE MILITARY BAND (*Playing*)
and CONFEDERATE CHORUS (*Singing*
"The Girl I Left Behind Me").

> I'm lonesome since I crossed the hill
> and over the moor that's sedgy.
> Such lonely thoughts my heart do fill,
> since parting with my Betsey.
>
> I seek for one as fair and gay,
> but find none to remind me.
> How sweet the hours I passed away
> with the girl I left behind me.

COMMENTATOR.
Delay was heaped on delay
as the rebels plodded along their way
in unfamiliar terrain—
country roads poorly maintained,
thickly wooded on either side,
and cut by creeks and swamps and deep ravines.
The afternoon of April 4 brought unexpected rain
pouring in torrents,
and continuing through the night,
flooding the roads, and impeding the march.

CONFEDERATE SOLDIER.
Here comes the most incredible part:
By morning, Saturday April 5th, the rain stopped,
and we marched two abreast,
General Hardee and his glittering officers out front,
all of us winding like a snake through the woods
to within a mile of the Federal camps!
By mid-afternoon of April 5, our line was fully formed,
batteries in place, everything ready for action.

CONFEDERATE MILITARY BAND (*Playing*)
and CONFEDERATE CHORUS (*Singing*
"The Bonnie Blue Flag").

> We are a band of brothers,
> and native to the soil,
> fighting for the property
> we gained by honest toil.
>
> And when our rights were threatened,
> the cry rose near and far:
> "Hurrah for the Bonnie Blue Flag
> that bears a single star!"
>
> Hurrah! Hurrah!
> for Southern rights hurrah!
> Hurrah for the Bonnie Blue Flag
> that bears a single star.

CONFEDERATE SOLDIER.
We had plenty of time the rest of the day
to enjoy the beauty of the dogwood blooms
filling the woods.

PITTSBURG LANDING

UNION SOLDIER.
On the morning of Saturday, April 5, 1862,
my regiment left Savannah by steamboat
and arrived at Pittsburg Landing by afternoon.
We moved up the bluff and into camp,
finding ourselves amidst the whirl

of an army in full swing—
men, cannon, tents, wagons,
mules and their swearing drivers,
drummers, darkies, peddlers, camp followers,
and the United States flag.

UNION SOLDIER.
The beating of drums
and the blowing of trumpets
fill my ears from morning to night.
Men are everywhere throughout the camp,
some in a pavilion playing cards,
risking all they had on a winning hand.
Moored on the river
is a fleet of steamboats.
All is hustle and bustle.
I suddenly saw a colonel,
and asked for the latest news.
He said he'd just returned from scouting
as far as seven miles from the river
and hadn't seen a sign of the rebels.

COMMENTATOR.
Either the colonel was blind
or he was confused,
expecting all the Confederates
to be wearing uniforms of gray.
Many did, but the rest wore clothing
of a mixture of colors and styles—
particularly butternut-colored coats and trousers
and farm clothing of every description,
and even outfits of blue.
To add to the confusion,
some of the Federals wore gray!

UNION OFFICER.
General William Nelson, the advance division of Buell's army,
arrived in Savannah at noon.
About 3 p.m., Nelson along with Grant came to my tent.
I told them my troops
were ready to march at once to Pittsburg Landing.

General Grant replied,
"But you can't march through swamps!
Make your troops comfortable.
I'll send boats for you early next week.
There'll be no fighting at Pittsburg Landing.
Our fight will be at Corinth,
where the rebels are fortified."

UNION OFFICER.
General William Tecumseh Sherman
encamped in a pleasant triangular piece of land
around Shiloh church, a one room log cabin
Southern Methodists had built.
They named it Shiloh
in honor of the first home of God's tabernacle.
Sherman's white tents are stretched nearly a mile
through the sparsely timbered woods.
Not far from Shiloh church is a peach orchard,
its beautiful pink blossoms in bloom.

UNION SOLDIER.
On the evening of April 5,
Colonel Jesse J. Appler sent a picket on reconnaissance.
About 4 a.m. in the morning of April 6,
the picket returned, and reported firing
by men in butternut clothing just south of the Union line.

Just then a Union soldier who'd been shot
came stumbling into camp, shouting,
"The rebels are coming!"

Appler sent couriers to General Sherman,
who dismissed the report with contempt:
"Take your damned regiment back to Ohio!
There's no enemy nearer than Corinth!"

COMMENTATOR.
Appler's report was the latest
in a series of reports to Sherman
that the rebels were approaching the Union camp.
Sherman dismissed them all.

Why?
Some say Sherman was smarting
from losing command in Kentucky
several months earlier,
when newspapers called him "insane"
for fearing that every rebel patrol
heralded a rebel attack.
It was not only newspapers who said that.
A northern general said
Sherman was "a splendid piece of machinery
with all of the screws a little loose."

All during the day
the Confederates, contrary to orders,
engaged in indiscriminate firing,
in the beating of drums, the blowing of bugles,
and the lighting of campfires
in scattered parts of the woods.

CONFEDERATE SOLDIER.
Many Confederate officers believed, with so much noise,
the surprise attack was up,
particularly General Pierre Gustave Toutant Beauregard,
second in command to General Johnston.

COMMENTATOR.
Although the Federal leaders were aware
of the Confederate presence,
those leaders refused to believe
that the enemy presence held significance!
After all, General Grant had said
there'd be no fight before Corinth, hadn't he?

Grant was so confident
all was peaceful and safe at Pittsburg Landing,
he returned to Savannah the night of April 5.
That same night, the Confederate army
made their camp just two miles south of Shiloh church
where General Sherman's Federals were camped.
At Savannah, General Buell arrived.
Having contempt for Grant,
and considering himself independent of him,
Buell did not notify Grant of his presence,
but set up in General Nelson's tent for the night.

CONFEDERATE OFFICER.
Around a campfire
our Confederate commanders
were having a war council.

General Beauregard wondered whether
they shouldn't call the whole thing off.
"We've arrived here two days late.
By now, Buell must have reinforced Grant,
in which case the Federals greatly outnumber us.
Besides, we've made so much noise,
there's no longer the element of surprise,
and the Yankees surely know we're coming.
And even if we drive the Yankees
all the way to the river,
they may still make a last stand,
repulse our troops,
and turn our victory to defeat."

General Braxton Bragg agreed with Beauregard.

General John C. Breckinridge,
stretched out on a blanket and gazing at the fire,
said that retreat now "will never do."

General Leonidas Polk was sitting on a stool
outside the circle, his head in his hands.
Then lifting his head, Polk said,
"My troops are eager to fight,
and the battle should proceed as planned."

General Johnston drew near, and said,
"Gentlemen, what does it matter
if they suspect we're coming?
We will fall on Grant like a hurricane.
But even if Buell's army has already joined Grant's
and we are greatly outnumbered, what does it matter?
I'd fight them if they were a million!
Gentlemen, we attack at daylight tomorrow!"

The plan was to attack in multiple parallel lines,
each corps in a line behind the other
and by sheer weight of numbers
drive the Federals into the Tennessee River.

COMMENTATOR.
It was Beauregard's words, so filled with defeat and doubt,
that were engraved upon my heart.

CONFEDERATE SOLDIER.
Although Albert Sidney Johnston
was our principal commander,
his generals and corps commanders lacked faith in him.
They said he was incompetent,
that he was much too kind
to be a strong leader.

COMMENTATOR.
Confederate President Jefferson Davis
had complete confidence in General Johnston,
and we've just heard with our own ears
how Johnston took charge
at the Confederate war council.

Nonetheless, many Confederates
pinned their hopes on General Beauregard,
the hero of Fort Sumter and the first battle of Manassas.
Those Confederates said,
"There's no hope in anybody but God and Beauregard."

However, Beauregard's defeatist words,
at the war council
certainly did not inspire hope.

As for General Grant,
his mind was made up
in spite of all the evidence to the contrary:
there'd be no battle before Corinth.

And so, Grant slept not in a tent like his army
at Pittsburg Landing,
but in a comfortable bed
at the Cherry mansion in Savannah.

At Pittsburg Landing, General Chaos was in charge,
and officers, lacking orders, just stood around.

CONFEDERATE SOLDIER.
We bivouacked in the tall trees
on the rim of tomorrow's battlefield.
All was quiet along the Tennessee,
except for the occasional tinkle of a cow bell
or the sound of a wild animal
moving through the underbrush.
It was a beautiful and starry night,
one of those balmy and delightful nights in spring.

UNION SOLDIER.
I was sent out as a sentinel.
I'd never been alone in the woods at night.
I couldn't help thinking
a rebel might suddenly steal up, and kill me.

SUNDAY, APRIL 6, 1862

COMMENTATOR.
At 6:30 Sunday morning,
across the river from Pittsburg Landing,
the sun was rising.

Pittsburg Landing is not a town
but simply a boat landing
by a thickly wooded region on the Tennessee.
Here the banks of the river are steep,
and a bluff rises a hundred feet.

Shiloh is the name of a rustic log cabin church
in a clearing in the woods,
about two miles south of Pittsburg Landing
on the main Corinth Road.

This little church serves
the farmers, the tradesmen, and their families,
but no one's going to church today,
neither to sing nor pray.
They've all been warned to stay away.

Still, some of Sherman's men
camped around the church are singing a hymn.

UNION CHORUS (*Singing* "Say, Brothers, Will You Meet Us?").

> Say, brothers, will you meet us,
>   On Canaan's happy shore?
> Say, brothers, will you meet us,
>   On Canaan's happy shore?
> Say, brothers, will you meet us,
>   On Canaan's happy shore?
>   On Canaan's happy shore?
>
> Glory, glory hallelujah,
> Glory, glory, hallelujah,
> Glory, glory, hallelujah
> Forever, ever more!

PITTSBURG LANDING

UNION SOLDIER.
At Pittsburg Landing
steamers loaded with Union troops arriving from Savannah
furnish our only entertainment.

The face of the earth is covered
with soldiers, wagons and teams,
and a long line of military stores.

Many men arrive with diarrhea.
A latrine big as an ordinary grave but half as deep
serves a company for barely three days.
Then the hole is filled, and a new one dug.

UNION SOLDIER.
One of the Illinois boys said
we'd have to fight in the woods,
but I didn't believe him.
How was it possible to fight in a wood?

COMMENTATOR.
Soldier, you'll soon see how it's possible!
More than 40,000 Confederate troops
with rifled muskets and bayonets
were stalking through the woods
toward the Union line at Shiloh church.

Although General Grant proclaimed confidence
he was not going to be attacked,
his men felt uneasy
from the signs of rebel activity.

Grant, too, must have been uncomfortable,
although he never showed it, for he wrote:

"Confederate skirmishing
was so continuous from April 3 on,
I did not leave Pittsburg Landing each night
until I felt sure there was not going to be further danger
before morning of the next day."

How could he be so "sure there was not going to be
further danger" with all that rebel activity?
What responsible commander
would leave his troops each night
for headquarters several miles away?

Grant also wrote:

"On the way back to the boat
to carry me to Savannah,
my horse slipped and fell
with my leg under his body.
The extreme softness of the ground
from the excessive rains
saved me from severe injury.
Even so, my ankle was so injured
that for the next two or three days
I had to walk on crutches."

And he returned to the comforts of the Cherry mansion.

FRALEY FIELD

CONFEDERATE SOLDIER.
Our orders were to take the Yankees by surprise
and attack at daylight, Sunday, April 6.
Each sergeant shook the men of his company
to waken them without making a sound.
It was 4 a.m. when we arose from our damp bivouac.
We'd already marched twenty-three miles in two days,
living on sodden biscuits and raw bacon,
and exposed to two nights of rain.
Our spirits were not buoyant.

Standing next to me was a boy of seventeen.
He pointed to some violets at his feet:

"Perhaps the Yanks won't shoot me
if they see me wearing violets,
for they're a sign of peace."

"A great idea!" I said, "I'll do the same!"
So we plucked violets
and arranged them in our caps,
while the men in our ranks only laughed.

Then, at 4:30 a.m., came the command,
"Forward, march!"
and our line began to move.

COMMENTATOR.
On the previous night, April 5,
Colonel Everett Peabody of the Federals
warned his superior officer
General Benjamin Mayberry Prentiss
that they were about to be attacked.
Prentiss mocked the idea.
Peabody was not the only Federal
to realize the woods
were swarming with Confederates,
and Prentiss was not the only commander
to discredit such reports.

Peabody took matters into his own hands,
and ordered a dawn reconnaissance patrol
under Major James E. Powell.
Major Powell discovered the Confederate army
in the woods by a cotton field near the Union line.
The field belonged to farmer James J. Fraley.

Fraley's field was a good lookout
for the Confederates to observe
Prentiss's and Sherman's camps
which surrounded Shiloh church.

At 6:30 a.m., the Confederates fired on Powell's patrol,
and soon both sides were firing away,
a clash that lasted from 6:30 to 8:00 a.m.,
when Powell's men were forced to retreat.
That unintended skirmish on Fraley field
began the battle of Shiloh.

General Prentiss was furious and asked Peabody
whether he'd deliberately provoked an attack
by sending troops to the enemy without orders.
Peabody said he'd merely sent a reconnaissance patrol.

Prentiss replied,
"Colonel, I'm holding you personally responsible
for bringing about this engagement."

Peabody said,
"General, I am personally responsible for all my actions,"
then defiantly mounted his horse and rode away.

Let's try to understand Prentiss's and Peabody's actions.
Prentiss was told by his commander,
General Grant, that there'd be no battle until Corinth,
which made it clear that Grant didn't want a battle
before Buell's army reinforced him,
for Grant's army numbered 35,000,
while Johnston's 40,000.

Peabody, however, concluded
that the Confederates were nearby and on the offensive,
and not defending Corinth as Grant believed.

Peabody's assessment was correct,
but his reconnaissance troops—
however unintentionally—
nonetheless provoked the onset of the battle
at a time when Grant's army was outnumbered.
That explains Prentiss's anger.

Peabody positioned his men
on a ridge under towering oaks.
Suddenly the Confederates appeared
on the opposite ridge.
They presented an awesome sight—
a seemingly endless line of men in butternut
coming through the oak trees,
their muskets glimmering in the dawning light,
and advancing like an avalanche.

UNION SOLDIER.
Our Colonel Peabody orders his men
to hold their ground,
but we are not organized and are greatly outnumbered.
A rebel battery opens fire with grape and canister
followed by a storm of missiles
screaming and shrieking though the air,
ripping through tents, smashing tent poles,
cutting off tree limbs that rain upon us—
and tearing up the ground around us,
raising a storm of blinding dust and iron hail.

CONFEDERATE SOLDIER.
We hear the order: "Fix bayonets!
On the double-quick!"
Our troops bound forward,
and break out into a yell so loud and so wild,
it drives away all sanity.
I have to say I enjoy shouting as much as the rest.
Nothing can stop us now!

COMMENTATOR.
Peabody's forces were shattered,
and they scattered.
He galloped back to camp,
looking for reinforcements, artillery,
and his commander, Prentiss,
when a musket ball struck him in the upper lip
and passed out the back of his head.
Peabody fell off his horse, dead.

SAVANNAH, TENNESSEE

COMMENTATOR.
General Grant was eating breakfast at the Cherry mansion.
Hearing cannon reports
from the direction of Pittsburg Landing,
he stood up and said to his officers,
"Gentlemen, the ball is in motion.
It's time to be off."

Grant, the Federal commander,
his headquarters nine miles down river from his army,
has decided to join his troops!
His steamship, the Tigress,
was waiting at the dock.

Grant boarded, sending two notes,
one to Buell, canceling their meeting at Savannah,
and the second to Nelson, ordering him to march
to the riverbank opposite Pittsburg Landing.

Grant, on the way upstream,
passed Crump's Landing,
where General Lew Wallace was awaiting orders.
The Tigress swung in close,
and Grant shouted to Wallace
to get his troops ready to move at a moment's notice.

But surely that was the moment!

Soon the cannon reports became more numerous,
and there was a continuous roar of artillery.

The Confederate commander,
Albert Sidney Johnston, on hearing the guns, said,
"Tonight we water our horses in the Tennessee River!"

PITTSBURG LANDING

UNION OFFICER.
A Union officer whom I'd never seen
suddenly appeared at Pittsburg Landing, and said,
"After the men receive their ammunition,
move to the top of the bluff and await further orders."

I said to him, "Who are you?"

He answered, "General Grant."

The men formed a line on the bluff,
but the officers, not receiving "further orders,"
galloped to and fro, not knowing what to do.
One officer cursed, as he wheeled his horse around.
He seemed to take consolation from a whiskey bottle.
That did not enhance his knowledge of the situation,
but it did increase the flow of his swearing.

Already there are wounded, many on stretchers.
And hundreds of Union soldiers are fleeing through the woods
toward the presumed safety of Pittsburg Landing.

UNION OFFICER.
We are still awaiting orders from General Grant.
He suddenly appears again and watches,
along with the rest of us,
his fleeing cavalry, artillery, and infantry,
all in a state of panic,
as they run from the woods,
and fly toward the river, shouting,
"We're already whipped!"

Infantry officers with drawn swords
try to head off the deserters.
And cavalry gallop after them,
threatening to shoot if they don't stop,
But no one stops.

UNION OFFICER.
Hundreds of Union deserters flee to the river.

Cool and undismayed,
General Grant suddenly gives an order:
"Officers are to return to battle."

COMMENTATOR.
If there was one thing about Grant
that impressed his men most,
it was his cool and undismayed demeanor.

Confederate brigades
under the command of General William J. Hardee
are pushing back General Sherman's Fifth Division
and General Prentiss's Sixth.

By 8:30 a.m., Prentiss's brigades
are in full flight to Pittsburg Landing.
They are a total wreck.

CONFEDERATE SOLDIER.
We load and fire, load and fire again.
My nerves tingle, my pulse beats double-quick,
and my heart throbs loudly, almost painfully.
I am angry at the man behind me;
the powder from his musket makes my eyes smart,
and I could have cuffed him for deafening my ears!

UNION SOLDIER.
As we began to retreat,
the rebels pour out of the brush
and into the open space before us,
shouting triumphantly.
Suddenly Colonel Peabody's horse passes by—
riderless, stirrups flapping in the breeze.

The rebels gave such a yell,
it caused terror to pass through us.
Once more we see their line of glittering steel
moving forward like a mighty ocean wave.

They close up
and move forward steadily,
inexorably.
Johnny Rebs are running from tree to tree,
and popping at us, one by one,
as they onward come
and come—
and come.

UNION SOLDIER.
The rebels fire a volley
that sweeps our front like a scythe.
Our horses fall with our men,
one great mass of flesh in a death struggle.
My own horse falls to his knees,
rises again, trembles for an instant,
then plunges forward, and rolls over on his side,
throwing me to the ground.

Someone shouts, "Every man for himself!"

Our line breaks, and like everyone else,
I run for the river,
all the while the howling Confederates
press in hot pursuit.

UNION SOLDIER.
As I rise from behind the log where I was firing,
I run as I see men in gray dashing through our camp.
I run faster!
As I passed our big mess tent, without any thought of food,
I thought of my knapsack with all my belongings,
including that precious packet of letters from home.
One backward glance quickly changed my mind.
But I couldn't help thinking,
what are they going to say about me back home?

CONFEDERATE SOLDIER.
We ran into the Yankee camp panting.
Seeing Yankee dead and wounded only half-dressed
showed what a surprise our attack had been.
Half-packed knapsacks with uniforms and bedding
of a new and superior quality
all littered the place.

One poor Federal shot through both hips
called to me:
"Please, I beg you, man, help me!
Help me!"

I said to him,
"First, tell me why you left your Northern home
to come down South to kill people
who'd never harmed you."

He replied, "Kind sir, I'm sorry!
And I swear, if you help me, and I survive,
I'll never do anything so foolish again!"

I said, "Take your case to a Higher Authority!"
and moved on.

CONFEDERATE SOLDIER.
Before me lay a fallen tree,
its trunk about fifteen inches in diameter,
with a narrow strip of light
between the trunk and the ground.
Behind this shelter
about a dozen of us flung ourselves.

The Yankee's cannon bellowed,
and their shells plunged into the earth
or rebounded
or flew with screeching hisses over our heads.
The sharp explosions and hurtling fragments
made us shrink and cower.
The balls beating on the log
sounded a merciless tattoo,
pinging as they flew off at a tangent
and thudding into something or other.
Here and there one found its way under the log,
and buried itself in a comrade's body.

A man jostled me.
I turned and saw a bullet had gored his face.

"It's getting too warm here, boys!"
cried a soldier,
"Oh, Christ! Oh, damn! Oh, shit!"
In so saying, he lifted his head a trifle too high.
A bullet skimmed over the top of the log
and hit him in the center of the forehead.
He fell on his face, dead.

Our officer shouted, "Forward!"

That command raised us up as if our feet had springs.
And in a second we were striding toward the enemy,
stopping only to prime the pan and ram the load down.
We raised a yell and sprang forward.
The yelling was taken up by thousands,
and we soon came in view of the bluecoats.
Their front dissolved, and they fled in double-time.
We gained their second line,
and continued to rush through them and clean beyond.

CONFEDERATE SOLDIER.
I was curious to see who the fallen were
among our Dixie Grays.
I checked on one.
He was stretched straight out,
eyes open,
and facing the scorching sun.
I will never forget the dead men with eyes wide open,
each with a fixed and infant's wondering gaze.

That square half-mile of woodland,
so brightly lighted by the sun
and littered by the dead and wounded,
was the first Field of Glory I'd ever seen.
Glory sickens me.
It makes me suspect it's all a glittering lie.

UNION SOLDIER.
Our fine corporal was killed by a cannonball
cutting him in two.
I was looking right at him when it happened.
After that,
all thought of saving ourselves disappeared,
and we all stood up, determined to avenge his death.

SHILOH CHURCH

COMMENTATOR.
After General William J. Hardee of the Confederates
drove General Prentiss from his camp,
Hardee planned to hit Sherman
camped in the clearing around Shiloh church.

UNION OFFICER.
General Sherman rides forward
to learn with his own eyes what's happening.
He still doubts all the reports that told him
the Confederates were coming.

COMMENTATOR.
It is hard to understand how anyone—
let alone a general—
could deny multiple reports
all with the same information.

UNION OFFICER.
Field glass in hand, Sherman surveys our troops
marching across the field.

A lieutenant runs up to Sherman, shouting,
"General, look to your right!"

Sherman drops the glass, and sees Hardee's advancing line.
The rebel skirmishers fire.
The orderly at Sherman's side falls dead,
whereupon Sherman,
as if awakening from a dream, exclaims,
"My God! We are under attack!"
Wheeling his horse around,
Sherman gallops to Colonel Appler, and shouts,
"Appler, hold your position, and I will support you!"

A PEACH ORCHARD

CONFEDERATE SOLDIER.
The Union battery is shelling us at a fearful rate,
and the order comes, "Take cover in the ravine!"

To our front is a ridge
and beyond it a peach orchard
with a field containing a Federal encampment.

Suddenly the opposite order comes: "Charge!"

We move ahead, slowly at first;
then picking up speed, we break into a run,
everyone yelling.
We pass right through the orchard
and the Yankee encampment.

SHILOH CHURCH

CONFEDERATE SOLDIER.
This was the first time in my life
that I was ever shot at, and I was scared—
well, I guess no more than the next man.

I personally knew many of the men
lying on the ground.
They were kinfolk, friends, neighbors.
My brother James was shot in the face,
but I couldn't stop to help him.
I saw Stephen Gordon.
There was no way I could help him.
Next I came upon Elias McLendon.
He was badly wounded. It was awful,
but I kept on moving.

Then our battery made a big mistake.
They thought we were Yankees,
and cut one of our men in two.
That caused confusion, and some fell back,
while others ran away.

UNION SOLDIER.
Within the thick wood is a vast clearing
containing Shiloh church.
From out of the wooded edge of this great opening
came regiment after regiment of Confederate troops.
The sun was just rising in their front,
and made their arms and equipment glitter.
I must say, it was a gorgeous spectacle!
The Confederates sprung into this field,
and, as they advanced, poured out their deadly fire.

UNION OFFICER.
We saw a line of Confederates marching,
and were just about to fire,
when General Sherman shouted,
"Don't fire! They're our own men!"
But the next moment, we saw the rebel flag,
and so we gave them the load of our guns.

CONFEDERATE SOLDIER.
As we entered the field,
we saw one of our regiments running away.
The officers tried to stop them, but it was hopeless.
The deserters merely brushed the bayonets aside
as they ran through our ranks.
Suddenly the Yankees opened fire,
and the rest of our men joined the deserters.

COMMENTATOR.
Not all the rebels ran.
Some of their units attacked Sherman,
and drove him out and into a rout.

UNION OFFICER.
I ran to Colonel Appler,
who was on the ground, behind a tree, and said,
"Colonel, so many of our men are running away.
Let's take their place, and charge."

He looked up at me as if I was crazy, and said,
"Absolutely not! Order those not deserting
to remain right here, and form a line where they are!"

Well now, here we are in the midst of a great battle,
and look at the miserable situation we're in!
Some of our men have never fired a gun,
and none have ever had a drill.
Our lieutenant-colonel has disappeared—
God knows where.
Our major is wounded and in the hospital.
And our colonel, the only remaining officer,
is a coward!

I said to Appler, "Dammit, Colonel,
I will not form a line back here!"

Whereupon he jumped to his feet, ran off,
and disappeared into the woods!

COMMENTATOR.
Was Appler the coward his junior officer said?
Hadn't Appler shown great courage
until that very moment?
Moreover, didn't Sherman promise,
"Appler, hold your position, and I'll support you"?
But Sherman did not keep his promise.
At last, finding himself in a desperate situation,
Appler runs away, and is called a coward,
while many Union officers, who also ran away,
were not in the least held accountable.

UNION SOLDIER.
The rebels were attacking on all sides.
They raised their cornbread yell,
charged, and captured our camp,
taking full possession of our tents,
our blankets, our knapsacks,
and even our love letters.

CONFEDERATE SOLDIER.
(*Singing* "Lorena").

> We loved each other then, Lorena,
> more than we ever dared to tell.
> And what we might have been, Lorena,
> had but our loving prospered well.
> But then, 'tis past; the years are gone.
> I'll not call up their shadowy forms.
> I'll say to them, "Lost Years, sleep on!
> Sleep on, nor heed life's pelting storms!"

UNION SOLDIER.
A colonel of the 6th Iowa shored up his nerves
with a bottle of whiskey.

When his brigade was ordered to retreat,
he alone marched back into the fight.

Our commander galloped up,
pointed at that colonel marching to the fray,
and asked, "What's the meaning of this?"

An officer responded,
"It means, Sir, the colonel is drunk."

COMMENTATOR.
Soldiers at the battle of Shiloh
frequently mention field hospitals.
As far as I know,
this is the first mention of field hospitals
in any military campaign.

CONFEDERATE SOLDIER.
Our men charged through a field by a peach orchard
containing Federals.
The boys in blue fired guns
when we were less than ten feet from their muzzles,
and so we were able to engage in hand-to-hand combat.

CONFEDERATE SOLDIER.
The ground is strewn with the dead.
Alongside a Federal soldier,
a beautiful Irish setter stands,
allowing no one to approach his dead master.

COMMENTATOR.
The Confederates increase their attack
on Sherman at Shiloh church.

UNION SOLDIER.
Some of us still make a stand by Shiloh church,
but there's lots of confusion,
and we're out of cartridges.
You see, there are six kinds of guns in our division,
and each gun requires cartridges of a different caliber.

Shiloh church is no longer a desirable place to be.
Bullets are coming at us from everywhere.
Our troops are retreating right and left.
One brigade runs like sheep.
I was about to fall back on my own,
when the order to retire comes from Sherman himself.
Three men approach carrying a badly wounded officer.
They call on me. I am a non-combatant—
a musician with the hospital corps—
so I complied.
As we carried the poor fellow along,
we saw our men fleeing in every direction.
The roads were packed with fugitives and wagon trains.
As soon as we placed our officer into a wagon,
I headed as fast as I could to the Tennessee River.

CONFEDERATE CHORUS.
(*Singing* "Wait for the Wagon").

> Wait for the wagon, wait for the wagon,
> wait for the wagon, and we'll all take a ride.
>
> Come, all ye sons of freedom,
> and join our Southern band.
> We are going to fight the Yankees,
> and drive them from our land.
> Justice is our motto, and Providence our guide,
> so jump into the wagon, and we'll all take a ride!
>
> Wait for the wagon, wait for the wagon,
> wait for the wagon, and we'll all take a ride.

CONFEDERATE SOLDIER.
A Northern woman, caring for her son,
begged for mercy.
I told her we were not out to harm
women or children or the wounded,
but only armed men.

We met ambulances and wagons
loaded with the wounded,
groaning and shrieking
as they were jolted over the rough road.
And we also met crowds of stragglers
to all appearances completely fit.

One of them asked,
in that whining way of deserters,
"Has you'ns been in the fight yet?"

By "you'ns" I thought he meant
some general or other, and asked,
"What troops does General Youens command?"

He looked puzzled by my question.
When at last I understood his meaning,
I shook my head and said, "No," and went on.

CONFEDERATE SOLDIER.
The roads are full of ambulances
on their way to makeshift hospitals.

UNION SOLDIER.
One man thrusts his foot forward
to kick away a piece of exploded shell,
thinking it had spent itself.
Instantly his foot's blown off.
A trembling rabbit rushes out of the brush
and snuggles up close to a soldier.

CONFEDERATE SOLDIER.
Our Tennessee regiment lays down for protection.
A Mississippi regiment comes charging through;
and as they dash over us,
one of them shouts,
"Move, Tennessee, and let Mississippi out!"
They run only a short distance,
only to return on the double-quick.
As they pass, one of our cocky Tennessee boys shouts,
"Move, Tennessee, and let Mississippi in!"

COMMENTATOR.
All day long,
General Grant repeatedly said,
General Lew Wallace and his reinforcements
were on their way.
But there's no sign of Wallace.
Where can he possibly be?
Lost in the woods?
Did he desert?

THE HORNETS' NEST

COMMENTATOR.
It is almost noon.
Prentiss's soldiers continue to retreat
until, by chance, they find an eroded old wagon road
on the side of a low hill.
It is here that General Prentiss
will make his last stand
at a place the Confederates will call
the "Hornets' Nest."

UNION OFFICER.
We were so near the enemy,
their cannonballs howled through the air
right over our heads.
So we left the main road
and filed along an old, abandoned road
that ran near the brow of a small hill.

The road was so worn down
that, together with the hill,
it formed a natural breastwork and trench,
the kind that General Grant was so certain
was completely unnecessary for us to build.
In this old road by the hill, we formed a line,
and were scarcely in position when the enemy charged.

UNION SOLDIER.
The land itself provides what our great commanders
so singularly neglected to provide—
an old worn-down road that serves as a defensive trench;
and a small gently rising slope
that serves as a natural parapet—
high enough and deep enough to give us partial protection.

A knoll behind us serves as a good place for our artillery.
Our front is also shielded
by an almost impenetrable growth of underbrush,
mostly of hickory and oak not yet leafed out,
enabling us to look out and take aim,
but dense enough to conceal us
until the enemy is within a few yards.
The Confederates call this naturally shielded place,
from which we attack
and so fiercely and repeatedly sting them,
the "Hornets' Nest."

COMMENTATOR.
General Bragg orders a Confederate brigade
to attack General Prentiss in the Hornets' Nest.
Then he orders another attack, and another,
and another—a whole series of attacks,
each of which General Prentiss successfully repulses.

CONFEDERATE SOLDIER.
We flanked the Federal battery
and would've taken it easily
but for a most unfortunate incident.

In the middle of our charge,
one of our young men galloped in front of our ranks
wearing the "Stars and Stripes" around his waist
and a Yankee cap upon his head,
both of which he'd captured as trophies.

Immediately a hundred guns leveled at him.
Both horse and rider fell, riddled with bullets.

At the same time,
another Confederate regiment
thought our regiment was Federal, and opened fire,
killing and wounding over a hundred of us.
Brothers killing brothers, friends killing friends.

COMMENTATOR.
Grant, in the thick of the fighting,
met with his division commanders.
He gave orders to General Prentiss
"to maintain his position at all hazards,"
for General Lew Wallace and his reinforcements
were on their way.

But Lew Wallace and his reinforcements did not come,
and the Confederates
continued to attack the Hornets' Nest
over and over again.
How long could Prentiss hold out?

CONFEDERATE SOLDIER.
The Federals did not fire
until we were within twenty yards of them,
and then the whole line with artillery,
opened up and mowed us down.
The roar of the incessant musketry and cannonading
made the ground shake,
and our men fell like autumn leaves.

UNION SOLDIER.
The rebels charged right up to the mouths of our guns.
And our battery fell into their hands.
Our colonel rode forward
and asked for volunteers to recapture the guns.
Instantly men sprang forward.
We recaptured the battery, all right,
but while doing so, almost everyone of our men
and almost everyone of our horses were killed.

UNION SOLDIER.
Charge after Confederate charge was repulsed
because of our sheltered position.
But as the day wore on,
our powers of resistance steadily weakened.

UNION SOLDIER.
It was hard to tell
when one rebel charge ended and another began.
And this went on during four hours.
We held our position, pouring out deadly fire,
and repulsing their every attempt to dislodge us.
The rebels fell like sheep to the slaughter.

COMMENTATOR.
The Confederates fall,
but the Federals are trapped.

UNION SOLDIER.
Under terrible rebel fire,
we were driven back into the ravine,
where we would load, crawl up, fire, and go back down.
Many men crawled up,
only to fall back, dead or wounded.
As I was loading my gun,
the man above me fell on top of me,
and rolled down dead at my side.
I kept firing until my cartridges ran out,
whereupon, my sergeant, revolver in hand,
placed the muzzle by my ear, demanding,

"Why the hell aren't you firing?"

"I've run out of ammunition."

"For God's sake, man, take the cartridges
from the dead man at your side!"

"Sir, my rifle is an Enfield
and his cartridges are for a Springfield!"

UNION SOLDIER.
The undergrowth was so thick,
we couldn't see rebels
until they were almost upon us.
We fired several rounds, but they kept coming,
and we knew we'd soon be their prisoners.
So we retreated.

A young soldier running by my side
gave an agonizing scream.
Then he began dragging a leg as he dropped his rifle
and fell on my shoulder.
I half-carried him,
while holding my beautiful Enfield,
but soon realized
I must either stop playing the good Samaritan
or drop the rifle.

I threw down the Enfield,
and set him down beside a tree.
I watched him as he continued to bleed in spurts,
but I knew nothing about staunching the flow of blood.
I called for help from a passing soldier,
but he gave no heed, and just passed on.

A second came by, stood looking for a moment,
and said, "He's a dead man," and passed on.
I stood and watched the poor fellow die,
and then I passed on, too.

Overwhelmed with thirst,
I saw a soldier with a canteen
sitting on a stump.
I ran over to him, and begged for a drink.
He said, "Help yourself!"

I took the canteen and drained it.
Warm water from a rusty canteen!
How delicious it was!
I'll remember that water for the rest of my life!

PITTSBURG LANDING

COMMENTATOR.
Union army camps are scattered about
without any tactical formation
or anything resembling a defense.
Who's in charge here?
What is the battle plan?
Does Grant have one?
If so, he's not sharing it with his officers.

UNION SOLDIER.
The steamboats at the Landing
are caring for the wounded, and transporting them.
Men are kept busy running with stretchers.
They're carrying out a man they say is dead,
but I can see he's trying to lift his head.

UNION SOLDIER.
I went to the river to get a drink,
the first I'd had for hours.
I saw an army of skulkers—thousands packed together—
hiding under the bank, not only ordinary soldiers,
but officers, too.
What a pitiful sight
to see so many men in a state of fright!

A cavalry officer carrying the United States flag
was riding back and forth on top of the bank,
entreating the deserters below:

"Men, for God's sake, for your country's sake,
for your own sake! Come up here,
and make one more stand!"
The only reply I heard was,
"That man sure is a good talker!"

COMMENTATOR.
At about 1 p.m., General Buell,
arrived at Pittsburg Landing,
and tied his boat next to Grant's.
He immediately went aboard the Tigress,
where he found Grant very anxious,
"without," in Buell's words,
"that famous masterly confidence."

Grant kept saying General Lew Wallace
would be arriving imminently with reinforcements.

Buell's attention was drawn
to the myriad frightened men
gathering under the bank.
And atop the hill,
he found nothing but chaos.

Buell encountered Colonel James M. Tuttle,
and asked him to inform him of the battle plan.

Tuttle replied,
"By God, Sir, I do not know of one."

TOWARD A PEACH ORCHARD
NEAR SHILOH CHURCH

CONFEDERATE SOLDIER.
About 2 p.m. our Commander,
General Albert Sidney Johnston, orders a bayonet charge
to clear out the Federals in a field by a peach orchard.
Johnston had given orders that he be in the front
and Beauregard in the rear.

UNION SOLDIER.
The rebels came on us in full charge.
Out of the ravine we poured,
running as fast as we could,
pursued by the howling enemy.

CONFEDERATE SOLDIER.
As the Union ran up the sides of the ravine,
our men at close range poured fire into their backs.
Many of them just lay down in the ravine,
not even trying to escape.
The bottom of the ravine was piled high with Union dead.

CONFEDERATE OFFICER.
As I reached the ridge of a hill,
I discovered our commander,
General Albert Sidney Johnston.
I joined him,
and we rode on together on the ridge
for about an eighth of a mile
toward a peach orchard.
Minnie balls were cutting branches
and striking the ground all about us.

I heard a ball strike
what I thought was the General's horse,
but I saw no wound on the animal.

Then I saw blood dripping from the heel
of the General's left boot,
the side on which I was riding.
I said, "General, you're wounded!
We'd better go down and under the hill,
where you'll not be so exposed."

Johnston said emphatically,
"No! We'll join General Hardee,
where the fighting's heaviest!"

One of his staff rode up and said,
"General, you're wounded.
I'll go for a surgeon," and dashed off.

A moment later, Governor Harris joined us.
Then, discovering that the general was bleeding,
Harris said, "General, you're wounded!"

Johnston replied, "Yes, and badly, I fear."

I was supporting the General on his left side,
and Governor Harris supported him on his right.
As we were heading down into a ravine,
General Johnston passed out,
and the reins fell from his hands.
We took him down from his horse,
and lay him on the ground.

His staff was present,
but no surgeon had yet been found.

General Preston was holding Johnston's head,
but from his awkward position became cramped,
and asked me to relieve him.

With tears falling on Johnston's face, I said,
"General, do you know who I am?"

His frame quivered and he opened his eyes
and looked directly at me.
Then he closed his eyes, and died.

There wasn't a dry eye among us,
and General Preston sobbed.
Dr. David Yandall, Johnston's personal physician,
was not in attendance.
On the previous charge,
Johnston, on passing a group of wounded,
some wearing gray, others blue,
ordered Dr. Yandall to attend them all, gray or blue.

Later we were told that the mortal blow
was dealt by a bullet
that severed the major artery below the knee,
and that a simple tourniquet—
a silk handkerchief twisted with a stick—
could have stopped the hemorrhage,
and saved the general's life.

COMMENTATOR.
Albert Sidney Johnston,
principal Commander of the Southern forces
in the Western theater of the Civil War,
died at 2:30 p.m., Sunday, April 6, 1862,
the first day of the battle of Shiloh.
General Johnston was the highest ranking officer
of the South or North
to die in the Civil War.

Governor Harris at once sought out
the second in command, General P. G. T. Beauregard.
Harris found him sitting on his horse outside Shiloh church.

When Harris reported Johnston's death,
Beauregard said, enigmatically,
"Well Governor, everything's progressing well, isn't it?"

UNION SOLDIER.
As I lay wounded in the field,
a Confederate came up to me and asked,
"Don't you Yankees have any land up North
on which to live and build your homes?
And so you had to come down South
and drive us from our homes and take our property?"

I was just about to tell him
we'd not come to acquire land,
but to stop the secession of the South
and save the Union,
when it occurred to me
he was as honest in his convictions
as I was in mine.
So I said nothing.

PITTSBURG LANDING

UNION SOLDIER.
At Pittsburg Landing,
I entered a field hospital, where hundreds of wounded
were being unloaded from wagons and ambulances,
and where their arms and legs were being cut off,
and thrown out the windows in gory and ghastly heaps.

UNION SOLDIER.
A great stampede is taking place at the Landing.
Thousands of deserters are trying to get aboard the steamboats.
This abominable mob has to be kept off with bayonets.
Disembarking troops insult them,
shove them, strike them.
The fugitives in the back crowd those in the front,
and hundreds are pushed into the river,
and scores drown.
As a boat pulls away, many spring on.
These crazy deserters express an unholy delight
at the certainty of our destruction by the South.

UNION OFFICER.
General Grant, as usual, was relaxed,
confident, and serene.

I said to him,
"Adequate reinforcements from General Buell haven't come.
Where is General Lew Wallace and his six thousand veterans?
I'm sure with those troops alone, we could whip 'em."

COMMENTATOR.
Grant made no reply.

The Confederates are resuming their attack
on the Hornets' Nest.
Confederates are yelling and shrieking
as they sweep across the field,
and are firing rapidly.
General Prentiss receives the full fury of the onslaught.
His line simply cannot continue to hold.

UNION OFFICER.
About three o'clock, our line almost melted away,
and our ammunition was nearly exhausted.
I knew if we didn't fall back, we'd be demolished.

General Prentiss said,
"General Grant ordered me to hold this position,
and that is what I intend to do
as long as I have one man left!"

A dread feeling came over me
that I was going to be that man,
so I walked away from it.

UNION SOLDIER.
About four o'clock our line dissolved into utter rout,
and I was captured.

CONFEDERATE SOLDIER.
How we are pressing them with our bayonet charges!
First one Federal drops, then another.
I hoop and I holler—and it's lots of fun!
All of us Southerners are happy.

The Union lines break and retreat in wild confusion.
We are jubilant! We are triumphant!
Our officers cannot curb us
and keep us in line for all our excited joy!
We fire and fire and fire some more,
pouring it on.
The Federals' dead and wounded cover the ground.

UNION OFFICER.
Rebel infantry pour through the gaps in our line,
and rebel cavalry pass over ground
only recently held by General Sherman.
Rebel lines can be seen
crossing a peach orchard to our rear,
thereby blocking the only road
where escape to the river is possible.

THE FALL OF THE HORNETS' NEST

CONFEDERATE SOLDIER.
A Yankee colonel sits on a fine gray mare,
looking at our Confederate advance,
as if we were on review.
One of our men rushes forward,
and grabs the horse's bridle,
telling the colonel to surrender.
The colonel puts the muzzle of his gun
to our man's face and fires.

At the same time, a ball strikes the colonel in the side.
He falls off his horse, dead, his boot caught in the stirrup,
his frightened horse galloping off,
dragging the dead man through Confederate lines.

UNION SOLDIER.
The rebels make another frightful assault,
from three directions, front and both flanks,
pouring shot and shell into our ranks.
The order comes to retreat,
and I run as fast as I can.

CONFEDERATE SOLDIER.
We came upon the Federal camp.
Our Colonel gave the order, "Charge!"
only to find that the Federals
had already stacked their arms and surrendered!
They even waved their caps and cheered us on!
We were certain the battle was over
and we had won!
The elation of victory filled us to overflowing!

UNION OFFICER.
About 4:30, the rebels' firing grows louder and louder.
They pour in by the thousands.
We realize we'd soon be surrounded,
and we, in the northwestern flank of the Hornets' Nest,
only await the order to abandon and retreat.
Will Wallace, our general, gives that order,
and men fly at a double quick to the Landing.

COMMENTATOR.
General Stephen A. Hurlbut,
commander of the southeastern flank of the Hornets' Nest,

had already ordered his men to abandon and flee,
and now General Wallace was doing the same.

Of the three generals at the Hornets' Nest,
Prentiss alone, centrally situated, held out to the end
as Grant had ordered him to do.
And yet, many years later,
Grant censured Prentiss
for failing to make a timely retreat!

GRANT'S "LAST STAND"

COMMENTATOR.
At Pittsburg Landing,
General Grant says he is making a "last stand,"
but I found no evidence of it.

UNION SOLDIER.
In the late afternoon
our chief of artillery is rapidly massing all available cannon
on top of the bluff, preparing for an assault.

About half-past four,
General Grant comes riding to Pittsburg Landing
accompanied by his staff and bodyguard
composed of about thirty cavalry.
He implores the deserters to make a last stand,
and redeem themselves,
assuring them that General Lew Wallace
and his reinforcements were on their way,
and Grant did not want his men disgraced.

He proclaims that if the stragglers do not obey,
he will send the cavalry to make them do so.
The stragglers do not budge.
Thereupon, the cavalry,
divided at either end of the Landing,
ride toward each other with drawn swords,
and drive every man up the bank.

Across the river we could see reinforcements on horses,
and soon the river was full of boats filled with them.
They must have been puzzled
at the sight of affairs at Pittsburg Landing,
its bank covered with bluecoats by the thousands
not engaged, idly standing about, doing nothing.
Slowly it must have dawned on them
what that dark and turbulent multitude really was—
a confused rabble of deserters seeking safety
by hiding under the river's bluff.

THE HORNETS' NEST

COMMENTATOR.
At the Hornets' Nest, the Union is collapsing.
Despite his earlier agreement with Benjamin Prentiss
to hold out to the end,
Will Wallace knew
that Prentiss would have no choice but to surrender.
The "Hornets' Nest" had held out for nearly six hours,
but could not hold out much longer.
Will Wallace decided it was time to go.
He had no intention of being taken prisoner.

UNION OFFICER.
About 5 o'clock, General Will Wallace,
having abandoned the Hornets' Nest and
while retreating with his men,
was struck by a bullet.
He uttered a cry, and fell,
apparently lifeless, to the ground.
The ball entered behind his left ear,
and passed out his left eye.
Three of us picked him up
and carried him a quarter of a mile or so,
when the firing became so hot we had to let him go,
and leave him for dead on the field.

The rebels converge and secure a crossfire.
We disintegrate and make a dash for the Landing,
while the Confederates cheer and yell
and shout in derision,
"Go, Yankees, go! Follow fast and follow faster!"
while their bullets execute the fleeing Union mass.

UNION OFFICER.
Over there stands a lone Union cannon
with gunners sitting in position.
Suddenly riders appear,
lashing their horses into a gallop
and passing by in splendid style,
heading toward the Landing.
Their uniform is slightly different
from regulation Union blue,
but attracts no attention.
They gallop toward the river,
then suddenly wheel,
shoot the gunners,

dismount at the cannon,
remove it from its caisson,
and begin to fire rapidly
into the mobs of fleeing Union.
Now we know who they are!
I have to say, it was a very brave act!
Although many of our Union soldiers rush by,
not one makes an effort to recapture the gun.

Rebels with muskets are so close
we can hear the click whenever they cock their guns.
Finally, surrounded,
we Federals had to give up our stronghold,
and started straightaway to the Landing,
but we had not gone two hundred yards,
when we discovered General Prentiss
holding high a white flag.

COMMENTATOR.
As General Benjamin Prentiss rode about the field
waving his white flag,
Southern regiments began yelling in triumph
at the sight of hundreds of Federal soldiers
standing or walking, hands up in the air.

General Prentiss raised himself in his stirrups
and loudly said,
"Yell, Southern boys, yell! You have the right,
for you have captured the bravest brigade
in the United States Army!"

UNION OFFICER.
At half past five o'clock,
on Sunday, April 6, 1862,

we soldiers from the Hornets' Nest
find ourselves prisoners of war.
Surrender took place just before sunset.
A Union prisoner loudly said,
"All prisoners are going to be shot."

Standing at my side was a boy.
He turned to me with large eyes and asked,
"Are they going to shoot us, Sergeant?"
I said, "No, son, they're not."

UNION SOLDIER.
When I got to the place where my regiment was,
I saw the men had stacked their guns.
I asked what it meant.
They said it meant we'd surrendered.
Those who understood were busy treating their guns
so they could never be used again.

Many a man who, until that moment,
had escaped harm, was now shot and killed.
Confederate troops fire into us,
and many Union prisoners are killed or wounded.
The rebel officer in command
told us to go into the tents.
We did so, whereupon heavy fire came upon us.
Believe me, one of the most dismal of sounds
is bullets piercing your tent,
without being able to see
where they're coming from.
And so, we went out of the tents.

CONFEDERATE OFFICER.
A courier brought me a dispatch for General Beauregard.
It reported that General Buell
was not rendezvousing with General Grant
at Savannah, Tennessee, as Grant expected,
but was marching in the opposite direction—
toward Decatur, Alabama.

I wanted to deliver the message as fast as I could,
and I expected someone to know the whereabouts
of Beauregard's headquarters.
I walked about looking for an officer,
but not finding one, I mounted my horse,
in search of anyone's headquarters.
I rode up and down in every direction
until I met General Pat Cleburne sitting on a stump
drinking coffee from a bucket.
He was as utterly in the dark as I was.
So I gave up, and went back to camp.

Near Shiloh church,
I chanced upon Beauregard and Bragg
sitting together in a Union tent
occupied only yesterday by Sherman.
With them was a great prize,
their Union prisoner General Prentiss.
I handed the dispatch to Beauregard,
who read it aloud, but said nothing.

COMMENTATOR.
General Prentiss said with a laugh,
"You gentlemen have had your way today,
but tomorrow it will be very different.

Buell will join Grant tonight,
and tomorrow we'll turn tables on you.
The information in your dispatch is false."
Beauregard was sure
Prentiss was trying to deceive him.

UNION SOLDIER.
My company's orderly sergeant was shot by a rebel
standing only a few feet away,
and who knew full well
that shooting a defenseless prisoner
was committing an act of murder.

Our general, Benjamin Mayberry Prentiss,
told the rebel officers
that if they didn't stop murdering our boys,
he'd order them to take up guns
and sell their lives as dearly as possible.

That stopped the firing,
but two of the rebel cavalry took our Stars and Stripes—
beautiful silk standards—and rode back and forth,
dragging our colors of Red, White, and Blue
though the mud.

Another one of our flags—this one made of cotton—
was torn to shreds, thrown in the mud, and trampled on.

CONFEDERATE SOLDIER.
This was one of the proudest moments
of my life as a Confederate soldier,
to see Federal gunners removing their artillery from the field,
Federal infantry lowering their colors
and stacking their arms,

Federal officers dismounting
and turning over their horses and side arms—
all the while Confederate officers
went galloping to and fro.
Unbounded and uncontrolled excitement was everywhere!
I myself was jumping up and down,
certain that not only the battle was won,
but the War was over, too!

CONFEDERATE MILITARY BAND.
(*Playing a spirited and full version of* "The Girl I Left Behind
Me").

END OF PART ONE

PART TWO

CONFEDERATE MILITARY BAND.
(*Playing a spirited and full version of* "The Girl I Left Behind Me").

THE HORNETS' NEST

COMMENTATOR.
As the first day of the battle of Shiloh,
Sunday, April 6, 1862,
was drawing to a close,
many Confederates were certain,
especially with the fall of the Hornets' Nest,
not only had they won the battle,
but they had won the War as well.

CONFEDERATE SOLDIER.
This was one of the proudest moments
of my life as a Confederate soldier,
to see Federal gunners removing their artillery from the field,
Federal infantry lowering their colors
and stacking their arms,
Federal officers dismounting,
and turning over their horses and side arms—

all the while Confederate officers
went galloping to and fro.
Unbounded and uncontrolled excitement was everywhere!
I myself was jumping up and down,
certain that not only the battle was won,
but the War was over, too!

UNION SOLDIER.
A big, burly rebel captain stepped up to me
and said, "Damn Yankee, give me your sword!"
Oh, how I wanted to give it to him!
But discretion prevailed, and I gave it to him hilt first,
thereby saving the burial squad two interments.

UNION SOLDIER.
I was under the impression that my nerves
the instant before my capture that afternoon
were as good as they'd been early that morning,
when I awoke fresh and raring to go.
But the moment I became a prisoner,
the whole day's work told on me,
and I wilted like a dishrag.

After surrendering,
I went right up to the Confederate line.
I wanted to see what kind of men these were
who could knock the wind out of us in an open field.

A Confederate sergeant stepped forward
and, to my surprise, offered to shake my hand.
Now I was wounded in the right shoulder,
and so I had to give him my left hand.

He instantly understood, put his gun down,
examined my wound, and said,
"It's just a graze; you'll soon be good as new."

I said, "You fellows fought like demons today."

He replied, "Yes, we're fighting for our homes."

At that moment, a great light dawned on me.

CONFEDERATE SOLDIER.
A Federal battery with horses attached,
and intent on making its escape,
faces us, and prepares to fire,
when our officer shouts,
"Yankees, boys, Yankees! Charge, boys, charge!"

Rushing at them at full speed,
and yelling at the top of our lungs,
they had no time to fire nor escape.
And every last man, horse, and gun was captured.

UNION SOLDIER.
General Beauregard asked General Prentiss
how many Union men were at Pittsburg Landing.

Prentiss replied, "If you want to know,
go there and count them yourself!"

Beauregard said,
"There's been too much fighting just in taking you.
In the worn out condition of my army,
I couldn't possibly go to the Landing tonight.
But in the morning I'll go,
and pick up the Union remains."

COMMENTATOR.
Tomorrow
Beauregard intends to clean up the Union remains!
Well, then, he had better get ready
and organize the Confederates tonight!
But Beauregard does nothing.

That evening the first of Buell's troops
under General William Nelson
cross the river to Pittsburg Landing,
but General Beauregard doesn't know—
or want to know.

UNION SOLDIER.
On reaching the eastern bank of the Tennessee River
across from Pittsburg Landing,
we found no transports waiting to ferry us.
When the first steamer appeared,
General Nelson had to force the captain to take us aboard.
Other boats appeared, but so crowded with wounded
they could carry only a few of us.

PITTSBURG LANDING

UNION SOLDIER.
Reinforcements ferried over on steamboats
were crowded on the lower deck,
while on the cabin floor the wounded lay in rows
as close together as bricks in a brickyard.

UNION SOLDIER.
The first boat brought over to Pittsburgh Landing
an officer of tremendous proportions
sitting on a Kentucky racehorse,
a magnificent creature with bobbed tail.
The officer was all decked out in his regimentals,
including a black feather in his enormous hat.
This *had* to be General William Nelson.
I ran down to where his boat was going to land.

As soon as the boat ran her bow on the sandy beach,
Nelson put spurs to his horse,
drew his sword,
and rode into the crowd of deserters, shouting,
"Damn your souls! If you won't fight,
let men pass who will!"

UNION SOLDIER.
I confess I was in the category of non-fighters,
a deserter, and so I asked one of the boat hands
to take me aboard.
After a little persuasion,
with the rubbing of his palm, he did.

As soon as I got on board, I climbed to the hurricane deck,
and was astonished to find my brother
among the reinforcements.
I gave him news of our father's death,
and asked him for something to eat.
From his haversack he brought forth a broiled chicken
and some hard tack.
I held a drum stick in each hand
as he and I marched off the boat,
up the road, and onto the plateau,
where I saw a man's head shot off by a cannonball.
But that did not make me stop eating,
for that chicken tasted mighty good.

Whereupon my brother turned to me,
looked me in the eye, shook my hand,
and told me to stay out of danger
and try to get home.
I readily accepted his advice.

UNION SOLDIER.
As I was lying near the road
leading up from the Landing,
I heard the strains of martial music,
and soon saw a corps of men in blue
marching by, playing and singing "Dixie."

UNION MILITARY BAND (*Playing*) and UNION CHORUS
(*Singing a spirited version of* "Dixie").

> I wish I was in the land of cotton,
> Old times there are not forgotten,
> Look away, look away,
> Look away, Dixie Land.
> In Dixie Land where I was born in,
> early on a frosty mornin',
> Look away, look, away,
> look away, Dixie Land.
>
> Then I wish I was in Dixie,
> hooray! hooray!
> In Dixie Land I'll take my stand
> To live and die in Dixie,
> Away, away, away down South in Dixie.
> Away, away, away down South in Dixie.

UNION SOLDIER.
The band was marching at a quick step.
I asked a young sergeant marching in the flank,
"What regiment is this?"
Back came the answer in a quick, cheery tone,
"The Thirty-sixth Indiana!
We're the advance guard of Buell's army!"

I gave a big gasping swallow,
the blood thumped in my throat,
and my heart pounded against my jacket.
In my entire, obscure military career,
never was the sight of reinforcements
so precious and so welcome.

UNION SOLDIER.
We Union of the Twenty-fourth Ohio
watched from across the river
as the Thirty-sixth Indiana reached the Landing.
Suddenly, we spotted a boat twenty feet below.
Down the crumbling bank we went,
slipping and sliding, or swinging,
holding onto roots and branches of bushes,
losing little time in reaching the bank and the boat.
Even the horses of our field officers somehow got on board.
And with overcrowded decks,
the little steamer headed for the Landing
on the opposite shore.

As we crossed the Tennessee in one direction,
we saw men in Union uniform crossing in the other,
making their way on logs.
How I wanted to shoot the cowards!

NEAR PITTSBURG LANDING

UNION SOLDIER.
I found General Will Wallace lying on the field.
He was alive, but unable to speak.
I intended to wait with him,
when a Confederate General came up
and promised that all possible care would be given him.
So I left.

CONFEDERATE SOLDIER.
We captured the Hornets' Nest,
and the news quickly spread—
and grew in the spreading!
Many of us Southern boys
came to look at the captured Yanks
out of curiosity.
Most of us thought we'd captured the whole Yankee army!
Then we found ourselves in the presence of a fresh brigade
of Federal infantry, a division of General Buell's army
just taking their position on the field.
They fired at us, but in their excitement,
fired so wildly and high, we were unharmed.

UNION SOLDIER.
Thousands of panic-stricken wretches
swarm the bank of the river,
a great mob in blue uniform—
a heaving and surging herd of humanity—
all smitten with the frenzy of fright and despair.

A little drummer boy stands pounding his drum furiously,
but to what purpose?
Some Union men stand wringing their hands,
and rending the air with lamentations,
while others cower behind the nearest object,
even the crouching form of a comrade.

Whenever a boat nears the Landing,
there is a great rush for it, some wading out breast deep,
only to be kept off by a bayonet's point.
Whenever reinforcements land,
there is a welcoming outburst of shouts and cheers:
"Glad you've come!"
"Good to see you!"
"Go to it, boys!"
"Give it to 'em, Buckeyes!"

while others pour out a different message:
"It's no use."
"The rebels cut us to pieces."
"I'm the last man left in my company."

COMMENTATOR.
On top of the bank,
General Grant, General Buell, and General Nelson
watch Grant's troops fleeing.
And every Federal commander is asking,
where is General Lew Wallace?

UNION OFFICER.
We have run out of ammunition,
and our only thought was of ammunition.

Near me was a Federal officer I did not recognize.
He was sitting on his horse
as majestic as a king on a throne.
I rode up to him, touched my visor respectfully,
and asked if he could direct me to the ammunition.

"No, Sir," he replied fiercely,
"nor do I believe you want ammunition."

I looked at him in astonishment,
not comprehending his meaning at all.
Doubting his sanity, I asked his name.
He replied in the same angry tone,
"What's the difference, Sir?
But if you really must know, I am General Buell."

Turning my horse about,
I rode to where I could now see
my men had found ammunition.
This time General Buell came riding up to me,
and in the same frenzy of wrath
demanded to know my name.

My answer was as insulting as I could make it.
"What's the difference, Sir?"
Buell interrupted,
"You haven't heard the end of this, Soldier!"
and rode off in a fury.

In a short while, Buell returned with Grant.
The two of them just sat on their horses looking at us
as we continued to fill our cartridge boxes.
Then we formed our ranks,
and moved forward into the line of battle.
Neither of them said a word.
And I never heard about the incident again.

COMMENTATOR.
Many fighting men on both sides
were fiercely independent,
so discipline could be a problem.
Sometimes privates and lower ranking officers
sassed higher ranking officers, even those at the top.
You see, farm boys are brought up to be self-reliant,
and do not always meet the standards of West Point.

UNION SOLDIER.
We were massed on the bluffs above the Landing.
Generals Grant and Buell rode along the line
and urged every man to stand firm,
for the Federal army could expect
thousands of reinforcements shortly.
They pointed across the river
to a long line of bluecoats as far as the eye could see.
It was Buell's army,
the only reason, in all honesty,
those of us of Grant's army could be saved.

UNION SOLDIER.
I was just about to desert,
when I obtained a swig of brandy
from General Grant's medical director,
who by chance was riding by.
That drink was the only thing
that gave me the courage to return to the front,
while many others went running—
stampeding!—toward the river.

UNION SOLDIER.
The steamers went over and back,
and over and back again.
A boat had to keep a slight distance from the Landing
lest it be swamped by the rush of soldiers clamoring to board.
Panic-stricken troops seemed completely insane.
An officer called to the cowering masses
to follow him to face the enemy.
I was stupid enough to do so.

CONFEDERATE SOLDIER.
Grant's army was crowded about the Landing
in disorder and confusion,
with just about everyone trying to flee across the river.
Men—and officers, too—sitting or standing on logs,
were making their way to the opposite shore.

CONFEDERATE SOLDIER.
We Confederates came to the bluff,
and saw the gun boats,
and thousands of disorganized Yankees.
But for some unaccountable reason,
we just stood there and watched
instead of dashing into them
and making short work of it
while they were in a state of panic.

CONFEDERATE SOLDIER.
With the last rays of sunshine
in which to deliver the final blow,
we were drawn up in the most magnificent line of battle
I ever saw—extending up and down the river,
to right and to left as far as the eye could see.

Every one of us understanding the situation
was eager for the signal to be given
to finish our glorious day's work.

COMMENTATOR.
But the signal was not given.

UNION SOLDIER.
We are facing west
and looking through openings in the woods,
where the sunshine falls bright on everything.
To the right and left, Confederate battalions are forming,
and their artillery getting into position.
Look way out yonder!
See the sunlight gleaming and flashing on the polished steel!
It is the coming of the enemy!
How distinct every rifle barrel, every bayonet and saber,
gleaming like silver, shimmering like brass!
We wonder, when are we going to raise the white flag?

COMMENTATOR.
I could not help but recall
the words from earlier that day
of the dead Confederate Commander
General Albert Sidney Johnston,
"Tonight we water our horses in the Tennessee River!"

UNION SOLDIER.
We are startled by a cannon shot above us,
followed by more.
Then comes a blinding flash and a mighty roar.
The earth trembles.

Suddenly, from the direction of the Landing
comes a deafening explosion
followed by others in quick succession.
Once more the ground shakes beneath our feet.
What does it mean?

Suddenly we understand, and we are exulted!
It is our gunboats pitching twenty-pound shells!
Still, the rebels keep firing,
their shots and shells hissing and screeching overhead,
or bursting into sharp jagged pieces
that come rattling down through the trees,
the smoke lingering amidst the leaves.

CONFEDERATE SOLDIER.
We lay down in line of battle
with the shells from the gunboats passing over our heads.
We wait expectantly to hear the order to advance and attack.
For this is the critical moment to capture Grant
and his disorganized army!

COMMENTATOR.
But General Beauregard gives no such order.
And yet, from his headquarters by Shiloh church,
General Pierre Gustave Toutant Beauregard
sends a telegram
to Confederate President Jefferson Davis in Richmond:
"After a severe battle of ten hours,
thanks be to the Almighty,
we gained a complete victory,
driving the enemy from every position."

Governor Harris asks Beauregard's permission
to size things up at Pittsburg Landing.
Permission is granted.
Harris rides rapidly toward the river
where he encounters a Confederate regiment
marching away from the Landing and to the rear.

Harris asks, "Where are you going?"

"We've received orders to fall back, Governor."

"Whose orders?"

"General Beauregard's!"

Harris soon comes upon regiment after regiment
marching to the rear,
all of whom say they've received the same orders.
Whereupon, Harris rides back to Beauregard,
and questions him.

Beauregard replies,
"Governor, you know as well as I
that our men have been engaged in battle
all day long, half with nothing to eat.
They need rest and refreshment.
It will take but a short time
to finish the operation in the morning."

Harris replies:
"General, by morning we'll meet the enemy,
perhaps with a different outcome."

CONFEDERATE OFFICER.
I was with General Bragg,
and heard him repeatedly say,
"One more charge, my brave men,
just one more charge, and we shall capture them all."

Bragg turned to me and said,
"We have to press our advantage
and finish the work before nightfall."

General Polk agreed, and said:
"The field is clear. The enemy is driven to the river.
Nothing is wanting but to press forward
and make a vigorous assault
on the demoralized remnant of Union forces
and complete this most brilliant victory."

UNION SOLDIER.
It was nearing sundown,
and our Union army was crouching like whipped curs.
The woods were alive with Confederates,
and, I must say,
in spite of the threat of our impending disaster,
a grander sight no man has ever seen
than the coming of the Confederate army.
Having the appearance of a huge monster
clothed in flashing steel,
the grays approached in perfect step,
arms at right shoulder shift,
their shell and shot making a thunderous roar.

The enemy's advance reminded me
of waves rolling in on the beach.
Yet, amid all this, Grant sat on his horse like a statue,
watching the enemy's every movement
as the wreck of his own army drifted by.
Then I saw the sun, a ball of fire, sink out of sight.

CONFEDERATE OFFICER.
A staff officer came up to General Bragg and said:
"General Beauregard has ordered
all pursuit of the Federals to cease,
that our victory is sufficiently complete,
so it's needless to expose our men
to more fire this evening."

Bragg said,
"My God, man, when was a victory
ever *sufficiently complete*?
Have you given the order to anyone else?"

"Yes, sir! And if you look to the left,
you'll see the order's being obeyed."

On seeing the retreating Confederates,
Bragg exclaimed,
"My God, my God! It's too late!"

Turning to me, General Bragg said,
"Captain, carry General Beauregard's order
to all the troops who haven't already received it."

PITTSBURG LANDING

UNION SOLDIER.
At dusk, by a smoldering fire on top of the bluff,
a group of officers gathered round General Grant.
Rain was falling,
and the ground was covered with water and mud.

Colonel McPherson rode up, and General Grant asked,
"Well, Mac, how're things going?"

McPherson replied, "At least a third of my army
is out of combat and the rest disheartened."

Grant was silent.

McPherson continued, "Well, General,
under the current state of affairs, what do you propose?
Should I make preparations for retreat?"

Grant's reply was short and quick.
"Retreat? Hell, no!
I'm going to attack at daylight, and whip 'em!"

THE NIGHT OF APRIL 6 –7, 1862

UNION SOLDIER.
At sunset Sunday, April 6,
dark clouds appeared in the west.
Lightning flashed and distant thunder rolled.
Hundreds of wounded and dead
from both sides, North and South,
lay strewn over the ground.

COMMENTATOR.
General Grant issued no orders.
General Buell on his own authority
decided to attack the next day at dawn.
Buell said, "I do not look upon Grant as my commander."

CONFEDERATE SOLDIER.
The sun was sinking when our Confederate regiments
retired from the field.
Happy Confederates sauntered along,
each with his share of plunder,
almost everyone with a gun besides his own,
and some with three or four.
Some had Yankee cheeses or hams on their bayonets,
others carried clothes and traps of every kind—
spoils from the Yankee camps.

UNION SOLDIER.
Under a steady rain,
I wandered along the river beach
when I came upon a soldier I knew,
and together we lay down on a bale of hay.
I soon fell asleep,
but every few moments,
I was awakened by a terrible broadside
from the two Union gunboats a hundred yards away.
Those black monsters spouted fire
all through the night.
I was also aroused by flashes of lightning
followed by terrible claps of thunder.
How I managed to doze I do not know,
but I did, and those naps were incredibly peaceful.

Buell's troops disembarked
some twenty feet from where I lay.
As soon as one transport unloads, it shoves off,
and another takes its place.
The tramp, tramp, tramp of Buell's army
comes marching past my bed of hay
to take position for tomorrow's battle.

UNION SOLDIER.
The roadway churned into knee deep mud.
I heard the slosh of marching men.
Now and then a battery of artillery disembarks,
and their wheels get stuck in the mud.
That creates havoc, and every man nearby
is recruited into push-pull duty.
The whipping of the horses and the cursing of the drivers
is far worse than the broadsides of the gunboats.

COMMENTATOR.
Beauregard slept confident of victory,
but not all the Confederates did.

Colonel Nathan Bedford Forrest
dispatched a squad of men disguised as Yankees
to infiltrate Pittsburg Landing.
They returned and reported
that the Federals were receiving heavy reinforcements.

Forrest promptly aroused General James R. Chalmers,
and said that the Confederates must attack at once
or quit the field,
for tomorrow we "will be whipped like hell."

Chalmers told Forrest to report to General Hardee.

Hardee told Forrest to report to General Beauregard,
but Forrest could not find him
in the torrential rain and black darkness.

By 9 p.m., Nelson's division,
the advance division of Buell's army,
was completely across.
Their arrival was met with loud cheering,
and by a band playing "The Star Spangled Banner."

UNION MILITARY BAND (*Playing the entire piece*) and
UNION CHORUS (*Joining in halfway through, and singing
reverentially* "The Star Spangled Banner").

> And the rocket's red glare, the bombs bursting in air,
> gave proof through the night that our flag was still there.
> Oh, say does that Star Spangled banner yet wave
> o'er the land of the free and the home of the brave?

UNION OFFICER.
To think we were nearly whipped,
when the arrival of Buell's army
presented the pleasantest sight I ever saw.

UNION MILITARY BAND (*Playing*) and UNION
SOLDIERS (*Singing* "Brave Boys Are They!").

> Brave boys are they!
> Gone at their country's call.
> And yet, and yet, we cannot forget
> that many brave boys must fall!

UNION SOLDIER.
We moved through the darkness,
not knowing where we were going.
Men were all about, but not a single camp fire.
The night is black. It is raining.
To keep together, we inch our way along,
treading on one another's heels.
Eventually, pressed together so closely,
we can advance no more.
So we fall asleep standing up.
When we awaken, remarkably refreshed,
we move again, striking our feet against the dead
or those with a little life in them.

These moan resentment
at being kicked and stepped on.
It's not as if we did it on purpose.
So we gently lift them aside,
and pass on.

UNION SOLDIER.
Wounded men ask for water.
Oh, the absurdity of it all!
Their clothes are drenched, their hair is dank,
and their faces are wet and cold and clammy.
None of us has any water to give,
but plenty is coming!
A thunderstorm violently breaks,
and the rain, which for hours had been a drizzle,
now falls in buckets that stifle them,
and we find ourselves
moving through torrents up to our ankles.

UNION SOLDIER.
(*Singing* "Little Major").

> At his post the "Little Major"
> dropped his drum that battle day.
> On the grass all stained with crimson
> through that battle night he lay,
> crying "Oh! for love of Jesus,
> grant me but this little boon!
> Can you friend, refuse me water?
> Can you, when I die so soon?"
>
> See! The moon that shone above him
> veils her face as if in grief,
> and the skies are sadly weeping,
> shedding teardrops of relief.
> Yet to die by friends forsaken
> with his last request denied,
> this he felt, his keenest anguish,
> when at morn he gasped and died,
>
> Crying, "Oh! for love of Jesus,
> grant me but this little boon!
> Can you, friend, refuse me water?
> Can you, when I die so soon?"

UNION OFFICER.
After midnight the rain continues,
and riderless horses come galloping through the dark.

UNION NURSE.
Work at the field hospital keeps us up all night.
We feed the wounded, pray with the dying,
and help carry out the dead.

Blood on our fingers,
blood on our faces,
blood on our clothing,
blood in puddles under our feet,
blood everywhere.

COMMENTATOR.
General Grant makes his headquarters under a tree
not far from the river bank.
His ankle is so swollen and painful he cannot sleep.
During the storm, he moves from under the tree
to the log cabin serving as a hospital.

UNION SURGEON.
In the log cabin, I noticed a general and an officer
seated together on top of two barrels.
A strange place for officers to sit!
I was even more surprised
to hear one address the other as "General Grant."
Both appeared dejected,
and there was little conversation between them.

Several times during the night nervous pistols were fired
by deserters just outside the building.
That greatly annoyed Grant; and once or twice
he left his seat on the barrel, and went to the door, shouting,
"Stop that firing! Stop it! Stop it at once!"
On returning, he said to his companion,
who turned out to be General Buell,
"The cowards! Were they to get what they deserve,
the first thing to be done in the morning
is to take a cannon and blow them to hell!"

COMMENTATOR.
Meanwhile, Union prisoners captured in the Hornets' Nest
are being moved south along the Corinth Road.

CONFEDERATE SOLDIER.
Poor Gideon Garret! Before going into the fight,
the boys of our regiment joked,
"Gideon, if the Yanks hit you,
we sure hope it'll be in the mouth,
for you're one helluva talker!"

And sure enough! A bullet passed from jaw to jaw,
but without doing him any harm,
except making a hole in each cheek
and knocking out three teeth.

UNION PRISONER.
After marching four or five miles toward Corinth,
we were hungry and tired,
discouraged and sick and mad.
I never saw so many long faces in all my life.
I gave thanks to God my wife is not a widow,
nor my darling child without a daddy.

Most of us lay down between rows of corn,
but we were too tired and out of sorts to sleep.
The night was chilly, but we had no blankets
or overcoats to keep us warm.
Still, a few of us were inclined to make the best of it.
One of our Confederate guards struck up and robustly sang
one of our favorite Northern songs,
which the South has now stolen as its own.
When he finished, one of our Union boys let him know
what we think of the South.

CONFEDERATE GUARD.
(*Standing and proudly singing* "Dixie").

> I wish I was in the land of cotton,
> Old times there are not forgotten,
> Look away, look away,
> Look away, Dixie Land.

(*Smartly sitting*).

UNION PRISONER.
(*Sharply standing and defiantly singing*).

> Away down South in the land of traitors,
> rattlesnakes and alligators,
> Right away, come away,
> right away, to the fray!
> Where cotton's king and men are chattels,
> Union boys will win the battles.
> Right away, come away,
> right away, to the fray!

(*Smartly sitting*).

COMMENTATOR.
After that, the Union prisoners decided
to let their captors have the last word on "Dixie."
So they sang a different song:

UNION PRISONERS.
(*Singing* "John Brown's Body").

> John Brown's body lies a-mouldering in the grave.
> John Brown's body lies a-mouldering in the grave.
> John Brown's body lies a-mouldering in the grave.
> His soul is marching on!

> Glory, glory, hallelujah!
> Glory, glory, hallelujah!
> Glory, glory, hallelujah!
> His soul is marching on!

CONFEDERATE SOLDIER.
You can't begin to imagine
how comfortably the Yanks were fixed.
They had Sibley and Fremont tents;
each man had two very pretty uniforms
and a large army overcoat, two blankets,
and an oil cloth to spread upon the ground,
cloth haversacks, and everything else
anyone could ever need.
They had large quantities of beef, coffee, sugar,
rice, flour, crackers, and corn meal,
hams and cheeses, apples and candy, and butter.

We also found a large box of greenbacks—
ones, twos, fives, tens, twenties,
even fifties and hundreds!
In addition to that,
they had all sorts of nicknacks—
paper, envelopes,
and some of the sweetest love letters!

UNION SOLDIER and CHORUS.
(*Singing* "Aura Lee").

  SOLDIER.

               Aura Lea, Aura Lea, maid of golden hair,
             sunshine came along with thee, and swallows in the air.

  CHORUS.

               Aura Lea, Aura Lea, maid of golden hair,
             sunshine came along with thee, and swallows in the air.

  SOLDIER.

             When the blackbird in the spring on the willow tree
              sat and rocked, I heard him sing, singing Aura Lee:
               Aura Lea, Aura Lea, maid of golden hair,
             sunshine came along with thee, and swallows in the air.

  CHORUS.

               Aura Lea, Aura Lea, maid of golden hair,
             sunshine came along with thee, and swallows in the air.

CONFEDERATE SOLDIER.
Our victory is so complete
that everywhere in the ranks men shout,
"The battle is over. The War is over!"

All we have to do tomorrow
is mop up the remnants of Grant's army,
which is ready to surrender!
The victory won,
half our army is moving back to Corinth.

Some of us ride on Yankee mules or horses,
others walk on foot, and some lay down on the ground,
the effect of Cincinnati whiskey.
Others are jumping up and down and whooping or dancing,
enlivened by Philadelphia claret!

CONFEDERATE SOLDIER.
Flashes of lightning rent the heavens
and showed sickening sights,
so I shut my eyes.
But through the dark,
I could hear the sound of hogs
quarreling over their carnival feast.

CONFEDERATE SOLDIER.
I lay on the ground.
All through the night gunboats and steamboats
were busy transporting Buell's army.
We could hear the ringing of the bells,
and the sound of puffs of steam from the boilers,
and the beating of the Union drums,
as Buell's army kept on coming.
Those sounds told us
we'd have a new enemy to fight tomorrow.
We were convinced
if we didn't defeat Grant before Buell arrived,
we'd have to retreat.

That night we heard many a shriek.
A wounded Federal called out to me,
"Oh, Southern man! Oh, states' rights man!
Give me a drink of water."
I went to him, and gave him a drink.

UNION SOLDIER.
I asked a Confederate to take me to his field hospital
and have the ball extracted from my thigh.
"If you do that for me, I'll give you half my purse."

He grinned and said,
"Yankee, under the circumstances,
don't you really think you should give me all of it?"
Then he laughed good-naturedly
and said, "It makes no difference.
Our hospital is full of our own."
Then he gave me some bread and water,
and covered me with a blanket.

Most of us Federals think the battle is lost.
Through the woods and over the fields
as far as the eye can see,
the Union line is in full retreat—
infantry, artillery, wagons, ambulances
all rushing to the rear—
creating a scene of an army in rout,
packed by the thousands with frightened men.

CONFEDERATE SOLDIER.
It was the most horrible night I ever spent.
A campground served as hospital.
The moaning and groaning sounded like a thousand frogs.

Part of my job was putting patients under chloroform.
I kept my handkerchief saturated,
and from the anesthetic's effect,
I often felt dizzy, sick, and tired,
nodding off and on the long night through.

CONFEDERATE SOLDIER.
Many of us Confederates had it good.
We got to sleep in Yankee tents and under Yankee blankets.
Many others, however, had no shelter from the rain.

It was a night of horror!
Flashes of lightning lit up the ghastly features of the dead.
And from their midst came the moan and plea,
"Water! Oh, a little water."
I heard it, but moved on.

UNION SOLDIER.
The surprise of the Confederate attack
was the result of gross negligence.
For the great loss of life,
General Grant is largely responsible.

UNION SOLDIER.
Grant's criminal carelessness
whereby so many brave soldiers were slaughtered
admits no excuse.

COMMENTATOR.
Dissatisfaction with Grant was widespread
among the Union troops and officers.
One soldier wrote,
"For the great loss of life, Grant is largely responsible;
it cannot be denied
we were taken by surprise."

Another soldier wrote,
"Grant must be regarded as an imbecile."

And it was reported
that many of the Ohio troops went about murmuring,
Grant should be "court-martialed or hanged."

MONDAY, APRIL 7, 1862

NEAR SHILOH CHURCH

CONFEDERATE SOLDIER.
An hour before dawn on Monday, April 7,
I awoke from a refreshing sleep,
and ate a hearty breakfast of biscuits and molasses.
I learned from the other early risers
that the South had won a great victory.
Our Commander-in-Chief,
Albert Sidney Johnston, is dead,
but General Beauregard is now in command,
and if Buell hasn't arrived,
we're going to win this day, too.

CONFEDERATE SOLDIER.
At daylight, as I started to rejoin my regiment,
I found two biscuits on the road.
They were soft as mush.
I picked them up and ate them.
I was hungry.

CONFEDERATE SOLDIER.
We feel we've already won!
So we load ourselves up with everything Yankee
we can lay our hands on.
For breakfast we feasted on crackers and meat.
I found a fine blue cloth suit,
entirely new, and fitting me perfectly.
The jacket had a pair of very pretty epaulets.

PITTSBURG LANDING

UNION SOLDIER.
Many of us sat on dead horses
while eating our breakfast of hard tack and raw bacon.
At our side lay six dead rebels
killed by a single cannonball.

UNION CHORUS.
(*Singing* "O Hard Tack, Come Again No More").

Let us close our game of poker, take our tin cups in our hand
as we all stand by the cook's tent door
as dried mummies of hard crackers are handed to each man.
O Hard Tack, come again no more!

'Tis the dying wail of the starving:
"O Hard Tack, hard tack, come again once more!"
You were old and very wormy, but we pass your failing o'er.
O hard tack, come again once more!

UNION SOLDIER.
We stand in ankle-deep mud
at the very place, some say,
Grant made a stand last night.

COMMENTATOR.
Hmmm. What stand did Grant make last night?

UNION SOLDIER.
As the streak of dawn appears,
the band of the 13th Regulars
marches from the deck of a transport onto the Landing
while playing a magnificent rendition
of "The Anvil Chorus" from Verde's *Il Trovatore*.

UNION MILITARY BAND.
(*Playing* "The Anvil Chorus").

UNION SOLDIER.
There is General Grant, his ankle so swollen
he has to be helped onto his horse.
His first order was, "Fall in, men!"
I couldn't help saying out loud,
"What? Before my morning coffee?"

UNION SOLDIER.
Some of us wondered whether our guns would fire,
after they'd lain on the ground all night in the rain.
"Bang! Bang!" began to be heard all along the line.

Grant shouted, "Stop firing!"

A plucky boy in Company C remarked,
"Does he really think we're going out there,
and shoot a gun that won't go off?"

UNION SOLDIER.
The patter of musketry on the river's bluff
told us the battle was on again.
Everyone was confident today's battle would be ours—
everyone, that is, but me.

I met a comrade drying himself before a fire.
He'd managed to secure a canteen
of commissary whiskey and offered me a swig.
I gladly complied.
That was my breakfast.
Cold and wet and depressed as I was,
that rot-gut brought me more consolation
than anything I'd ever drunk before.

UNION SOLDIER.
The house at the top of the hill
served as an amputation room.
Limbs were tossed out of one of the windows,
and before long there was a pile five feet high.

COMMENTATOR.
Today
Beauregard is expecting to conquer Grant's battered army.
But Beauregard, whose judgment seems impaired,
is in for a surprise.
His Confederate army is disorganized,
and without reinforcements.
With only about 25,000 troops remaining,
they are unprepared for what they're about to face.

By 8 a.m. General Buell
had nearly 15,000 fresh Union men on the field,
and—lo and behold!—General Lew Wallace
suddenly appeared with about 6,000.
Lew Wallace at last! Where has he been?

Grant had refused to send Wallace written orders,
but sent him verbal ones instead.
What message did Grant send?
What message did the courier deliver?
No one will ever know.
The essential message
must have gone something like this:
Wallace, march to Pittsburgh Landing.

But the route Wallace took was strange,
not the most direct,
but a wandering way in the deep woods,
and it took Wallace an exceedingly long time
to get to his destination,
by which time the battle was almost over.

Nonetheless, with Wallace's reinforcements
added to Grant's and Buell's armies,
the Federals are now attacking with about 45,000 troops,
nearly twice as many as the Confederates.

CONFEDERATE SOLDIER.
Our force was disorganized, demoralized, exhausted,
but above all, we were out of ammunition.

And though millions of cartridges
were stacked along side our officers,
not one officer in ten thought to supply his men—
so confident were they of victory.

CONFEDERATE SOLDIER.
As our unit retreats,
a wild eyed rider gallops by,
warning us to run for our lives,
for Buell has arrived, and completely surrounded us.

UNION SOLDIER.
The rebels are coming at us like devils.
We pour out volley upon volley,
and soon there are only dead and wounded Butternuts.

CONFEDERATE SOLDIER.
A fellow Confederate soldier said,
"Where is my regiment?
I want to be with my regiment!"

"Never mind! Fall in here! Fall in there!
Fall in *anywhere*!"
came an officer's response.

CONFEDERATE OFFICER.
I am not a field officer;
even so I am a captain simply because I'm an engineer.
We didn't have a field officer among us,
and so, I appointed myself one.
I gathered and organized about a thousand men,
who came from half a dozen different regiments.
I divided the troops into companies,
and appointed another non-field officer as major.

CONFEDERATE SOLDIER.
Commands kept getting mixed up.
So, men in the front
were fired upon by men in the rear,
and pandemonium prevailed.

I made my way to Shiloh church,
and found General Beauregard with his staff.
Just as I arrived, a courier rode up
with a message Beauregard couldn't understand.

UNION PRISONER.
The Confederates went through the motions of feeding us.
They gave us a small piece of raw pork on a moldy cracker.

We had scarcely swallowed that delicacy,
when the whole gang of Butternuts
suddenly became terribly excited.
Their cavalry were flying about us,
and a double line of guards were stationed all around us.
We were sure that in that state of agitation,
they were going to fire on us.
Luckily that didn't happen.

But while this was going on,
I saw a club on the ground.
It occurred to me to run and grab it,
and, by swinging, make my way
through their lines to the river.
Before I could carry out this dumb plan,
we were hurried onto the Corinth road.

A PEACH ORCHARD

UNION SOLDIER.
Our Union regiment halted,
and I heard a voice calling,
"Oh, friend! You, there!
For God's sake, come here!"

I went to where I heard the voice,
and came to a gory pile of dead
in every kind of stiff contortion.
I saw an arm slowly raise and beckon me,
and I went to the place,
where I found a rebel pillowing his head
on a dead comrade's body.
Both were colored red from head to foot.
The dead man's brains had gushed out
in a reddish and grayish mass over his face.

The live one had been laying across him
all that horrible, long, and stormy night.
He said to me,
"O God, what made you Yankees
come down south to fight us?
We'd never go up north to fight you!"
And then he put an arm affectionately
over the body of his dead comrade,
and laid his bloody face
against the cold, clammy, bloody face of his friend.

Then came my Colonel's command,
"Forward!"

"Forward!"
repeated my officer.

Forward
I went.

UNION SOLDIER.
Knapsack and haversack were distended
with soaked and swollen biscuits;
rifles lay with bent barrels or splintered stocks;
hats and blankets were beaten into the mud by the rain;
and the omnipresent sardine box littered the spongy earth
as far as the eye could see.

Dead horses were everywhere,
and ammunition wagons stood desolate
behind four or six sprawling mules.

Near where I halted my platoon,
a Union sergeant lay, his face upward,
breathing in convulsive, rattling snorts,
and blowing out in sputters white froth,
which crawled creamily down his cheeks,
piling itself alongside his neck and ears.
A bullet had clipped his skull
from which the brain protruded.

One of my men asked
if he should put his bayonet through him.
I was shocked at that proposal,
and told him I thought not,
for it was an unusual thing to do.
Besides, too many men were watching.

UNION SOLDIER.
By 10 a.m., the rebel enemy was driven back.
The pallid faces of the dead in blue
were scattered among
the blackened corpses of the dead in gray.
All bodies had been stripped of valuables.
Scarcely a pair of boots or shoes covered their feet,
and the pockets were slashed open.

ALONG THE CORINTH ROAD

CONFEDERATE SOLDIER.
Our troops are moving south on the Corinth road.
Knowing that our Southern army is victorious,
we are at a loss to explain our retreat.

CONFEDERATE SOLDIER.
In front and on both our flanks, I see Yankees!
The very earth swarms with them!

CONFEDERATE SOLDIER.
Men drop on both sides like slaughtered animals.
Raising my gun, I take aim and fire.
As I was reloading,
a ball came crashing through my canteen.
As the warm liquid poured out,
I was certain my blood was gushing from a mortal wound,
and I started to look for a surgeon.
On arriving at a hospital tent,
I was happy to learn that my life had been saved
by the self-sacrificing heroism of my canteen!

CONFEDERATE SOLDIER.
We stood in the woods behind a cotton field.
The Federals were in the woods on the opposite side.
The command to charge was given,
but it was hopeless to drive back Buell's troops,
for they were fresh,
so we ran back into the woods.

Finally, our officers were convinced
further charges were futile,
and ordered our retreat.
Whereupon,
one of our privates went running into the field,
waving his hat and shouting,
"I am fighting for our country!
Damn you all, for not fighting for your country!"

CONFEDERATE SOLDIER.
During one of our charges,
we came across a wounded Federal
making an effort to shoot us.
As we turned to shoot him,
he threw down his gun, and threw up his hands.
So we passed him by, and let him be.
Unexpectedly, he picked up his gun and fired,
seriously wounding one of our men.
Whereupon, we shot him to hell.

CONFEDERATE SOLDIER.
General Beauregard was as surprised as anyone
when the Federals attacked us.
Nevertheless, he plunged into the fight
cheerfully and energetically.

He rode up to us with a smile,
looking as cool and collected,
amid the hailstorm of minnie balls,
as if he were in a drawing room sipping tea.

Doffing his hat, he said,
"Men, the day is ours!
You are fighting a whipped army!"

With encouragement like that
from the Commander-in-Chief,
how could we lose?
So we gave three cheers,
and rushed into the bloody fray.

COMMENTATOR.
As the day wore on,
Beauregard's countenance changed;
but he never once admitted
that his worn out army was losing.

CONFEDERATE SOLDIER.
We jump behind whatever tree is near,
then fire, load, and dart to another tree.
I am so absorbed with the Blues,
I pay no attention to the whereabouts
of my fellow Grays.
Suddenly, I rise to discover I'm the only Gray!
The rest have run away!

Next I hear, "Down with the gun, Secesh,
or I'll drill a hole in your head!"

And half a dozen Blues are on me.
I drop my gun.
I am a Yankee prisoner!

A burst of vituperations in a German accent
comes from several Yankee throats.
Their voices are loud:

"Vy do you bodder to take him?
Vy don't you shtick a bayonet into dot shvinehunt,
and let him drop right ver y is!"

This and other things they shout
as they grow more and more excited
until a few of them rush at me with leveled bayonets,
their faces deformed with fury, their eyes bulging.

Before the bayonets reach me,
two of my guards, ruddy-faced Northerners from Ohio,
fling themselves in front of me.
They present rifles and shout,
"There now, you men, stop that at once!
He's our prisoner!"

At the same time, a couple of officers
flourishing swords, shout,
"Damn you, men! Behave!"
That drove them back into the ranks.

CONFEDERATE SOLDIER.
These troops are Buell's,
and what an imposing sight they are!
New uniforms and shiny brass buttons!

They came nearer to my idea of a soldier
than did our dingy gray troops.
Still in all, they lacked the lean boldness
and confidence
of us men of the South.

My guards and I eventually
came to a discussion of our respective causes.
And although I'd never admit it,
there was much reason in what they said.

Until then, I was under the impression
that the Northerners were robbers,
who only sought to desolate the South
and steal our slaves.

But according to them,
if we hadn't been so impulsive and flown to arms,
it might have been possible for Congress
to compensate slave-owners,
buy up all the slaves, and only then set them free.

But when we Southerners
began to seize government property—
forts, arsenals, warships—
and set up a separate government, dividing the Union,
the North resolved this could never be.
And that was the true reason for the war.

At the riverside was tremendous activity.
In one place on the slope
Confederate prisoners stood in a corral.
I was handed over to the guards.

ON THE ROAD TO CORINTH, LATE THAT AFTERNOON

UNION PRISONER.
The roads are bad, in places barely passable.
We prisoners have to wade through knee deep mud.
The woods are full of rebels.
Many are deserters.

CONFEDERATE SOLDIER.
I meet hundreds of our Southern boys walking away
with packed Yankee knapsacks.
When I ask them if they're wounded,
they say, "No. I'm sick,"
while carrying a load on their backs
I couldn't carry if I were well.

UNION PRISONER.
Our rebel guards were uneasy
the whole time they were hurrying us along.
Whenever their couriers overtook us,
we could tell they felt all was not well.

The firing picked up to our rear,
which told us General Grant and General Buell
were on the march.
Once or twice our guards became agitated
by reports that the Yankee cavalry was in pursuit,
intent on freeing us prisoners.

COMMENTATOR.
That was erroneous thinking
on the part of the Confederate captors,
and wishful thinking
on the part of the Union prisoners.
For neither Grant nor Buell gave a thought
to recapturing the prisoners and setting them free.
Defeated and depressed,
the Confederates, nonetheless,
made a last stand at Shiloh church.

UNION SOLDIER.
For the first time I heard the rebel yell,
faintly at the start, but growing louder
as it's taken up by rebels all along the line
until it became a great pandemonium.
On they come!

The thought crossed my mind
that the hand of death was hovering over me.

Just then it felt as if a hot cannonball
struck me on the head, and I passed out.
When I came to,
I heard the men around me saying,
"No use taking him off the field.
Look at his head!"
I began to feel more and more faint,
when a corpsmen took me away in an ambulance.

CONFEDERATE SOLDIER.
I'm beginning to have my doubts
as to the outcome of this contest.
We can't hold out much longer.

So our Southern boys retreat, at first one by one,
then whole squads,
then whole regiments!

COMMENTATOR.
A little after two o'clock,
Governor Isham Harris took Colonel Thomas Jordan aside,
and said, "Colonel, don't you think the day's going against us?
And isn't there danger in tarrying so long in the field?"

Jordan replied, "I agree. Retreat is the proper course."

A moment later, having the opportunity
to speak to General Beauregard alone,
Jordan said to him, "General, don't you think
our troops are like a lump of sugar
thoroughly soaked with water,
still preserving its original shape, but ready to dissolve?
And so, wouldn't it be judicious to get away?"

Beauregard, calling his aides-de-camp,
dispatched them with orders to begin the retreat.
He then directed Jordan,
"Collect as many of the broken regiments as you can.
Post them in the best position, and hold it
until the whole army passes by."

Jordan, with his force of about two thousand infantry
and a dozen or so cannon, quickly found such a position
on an elevated ridge overlooking Shiloh church.
Here they remained until a little after four p.m.,
when the last of the Confederates filed past,
whereupon they, too, fell in line
and began the march back to Corinth.

General Bragg found quitting "sad beyond measure."
He refused to believe the order
before sending a message to Beauregard
confirming that the directive was correct.
By 3:30, full retreat had begun.

General Grant's ankle was so swollen,
he had to be lifted in and out of the saddle.
I think he was glad to see the Butternuts go,
and saw no need to pursue them.
No need to pursue them!

General Grant, haven't you forgotten
General Prentiss?
He is being held prisoner by the Butternuts.
And haven't you forgotten the Union troops
who fought so valiantly at the Hornets' Nest?
They, too, are prisoners,
and are marching to Corinth.
Do you intend to abandon them?

I guess he does.

UNION SOLDIER.
We Federals were too tired to advance.
Our line halted every now and then,
and our tired boys dozed;
despite my best efforts to stay awake, I dozed, too.
A battery of Parrott guns fired overhead.
Even that failed to rouse us,
and get us moving.

But suddenly joyous shouts of victory
from our Federal boys filled the air,
and we suddenly woke up
and advanced quickly.

UNION SOLDIER.
As Confederates were retreating,
I couldn't help thinking,
How appalling the change wrought in a single day!
Yesterday they were winning.
Today they are defeated.

Fences are leveled,
fields of sprouting grain trodden underfoot,
thickets on fire,
trees torn and splintered as if by a mighty storm,
muskets broken and trampled into the blood stained mire,
tents overturned, artillery abandoned,
and the dead and dying—horses as well as men—
scattered everywhere,
while the plaintive cries of the wounded
send a chill of horror through the bravest heart.

UNION SOLDIER.
In one tent I found a bright young rebel,
merely a boy, badly wounded.
I saw to it he was carried to a hospital.

Another wounded beardless rebel boy,
about fourteen or fifteen, asked,
"What you-uns come down to fight we-uns for?
If you want the niggers, I wished you had 'em all.
I ain't got any."

PITTSBURG LANDING

UNION VOLUNTEER NURSE.
Two fine ladies from a steamboat
wanted "to do something."
So I got some buckets and took them to a place
where there'd just been fighting.
The dead and dying lay thick around us.
One of the ladies fainted.
The other bore it well,
and she and I filled our buckets from a spring,
and gave the thirsty water to drink.

Then we tore our aprons into small squares
and filled them with grass and leaves;
and with these plugs
filled some gaping wounds,
and stanched the bleeding.

We made bandages from our garments,
and as best we could, bound up shattered limbs.
Ambulances were busy carrying men
to the old house on the hill,
where knife and saw were busy
doing their bloody work.

Men were begging for water.
Some were crying, "I want my mother!"
Others cried, "I want to go home to my wife!"

UNION SOLDIER.
About 3 o'clock, the firing
from south of Shiloh Church
seemed to slacken and be more distant.
Soon the glad news came:
"The rebel enemy is retreating!"
Every Union coward who'd slunk under the river bank
now came out of his hole.

COMMENTATOR.
Colonel Jordan's rebels were in the woods near Shiloh church.
That was the same position Sherman held
when the battle began only yesterday morning.

Some of Buell's troops arrived on the field.
After a fierce fight of about thirty minutes,
the rebels were driven from their position,
and fell back on the Corinth road,
their main force already in full retreat.
That was the Confederates' last stand,
meant to cover their main force's retreat.
Jordan's retreat brought the battle of Shiloh to an end.

General Buell did not pursue the retreating foe,
but ordered his troops into camp.
A competent commander would have pursued
this beaten, demoralized, and fleeing enemy,
if only to free the five thousand Union prisoners.

CONFEDERATE SOLDIER.
Along a narrow and almost impassable road,
was a line of wagons
loaded with wounded, piled in like bags of grain,
groaning and cursing,

while the mules plunged on in belly deep water
that sometimes came into the wagons.
We met hundreds of men hit in every part of the body,
but mostly in the arms and hands.

CONFEDERATE SOLDIER.
The wounded were jostled along over the rough road
in springless wagons.
Some groaned; many died during that awful retreat,
and their bodies were thrown out
to make room for the living.

CONFEDERATE SOLDIER.
The cold, drizzling rain came harder and faster,
then turned to pitiless hail,
which fell in stones as large as partridge eggs.

I drove an army wagon all night.
Every few minutes a courier'd come riding up and say,
"Drive faster! The Yanks are pressing us hard."

COMMENTATOR.
But it wasn't true. The Yanks were not in pursuit.

UNION SOLDIER.
One of our surgeons said,
"The agonies of the wounded are beyond description.
Imagine two to three thousand
calling to have their wounds dressed.

We worked as best we could,
but the crowded conditions and large numbers,
and the complete absence of preparations
by our commander for such an event,
caused a great deal of suffering
that could have been prevented."

Everett Peabody was found where he'd fallen,
the buttons and shoulder straps
cut from his uniform, his sword and pistols gone.
His men buried him, marking the spot with a board
on which they scrawled:
"A braver man ne'er died upon the field."

TUESDAY, APRIL 8, 1862, AND THE DAYS THAT FOLLOWED

COMMENTATOR.
Dawn on Tuesday morning, April 8, revealed
in every direction as far as the eye could see,
those who fell.

UNION COMMANDING OFFICER.
Wagons are hauling dead men
and dumping them like cordwood
for burial in long trenches
like sardines in a box.

CONFEDERATE SOLDIER.
I captured me a mule.
Now he was not a fast mule, and he was contrary.
If I wanted him to go on one side of the road,
he was sure to go on the other.
So I got myself a hickory stick,
and flailed him over the head.
But he'd only shake his head and flop his ears.
Me and the mule worried along
until we came to a creek.
Mule did not desire to cross,
despite my persuasion with the stick,
a rock to his ear,
and a twist of his nose.

A caisson came up
and promptly crossed the creek.
The driver halted and said,
"I'll get your mule to cross."
So he got a large two inch rope,
tied one end round the mule's neck
and the other to the caisson,
and got the caisson moving again.

Rope began to tighten around mule's neck,
and mule began to squeal in protestation
against such villainous proceedings.
Rope, however, was stronger than mule,
who was finally prevailed upon to cross the creek.

I mounted mule again—
when all of a sudden
he lifted his head,
pricked up his ears,
began to chomp at the bit,
gave a little squeal,
started to move,
and then flew into a gallop.
With all my pulling
and seesawing and strength
and shouting of "Whoa!"
I couldn't stop him
until we galloped into Corinth!

COMMENTATOR.
Not all Confederates were retreating.
The rear guard continued to occupy the battlefield,
not to fight, but to gather trophies of defeat,
while the Federals gathered trophies of victory.
The two sets of trophies were the same.

CONFEDERATE SOLDIER.
Details of men are busy all day
gathering, burning, and burying the dead,
our dead and theirs.

CONFEDERATE SOLDIER.
(*Singing* "Weeping Sad and Lonely [When This Cruel War is Over]").

> Weeping, sad and lonely,
> sighs and tears how vain!
> When this cruel war is over,
> praying that we meet again.
>
> When the summer breeze is sighing
> mournfully along,
> or when autumn leaves are falling,
> sadly breathes the song.
> Oft in dreams I see thee lying
> on the battle plain
> lonely, wounded, even dying,
> calling but in vain.
>
> Weeping, sad and lonely,
> sighs and tears how vain!
> When this cruel war is over,
> praying that we meet again.

UNION SOLDIER.
A hundred fires are in full blast at the same time,
as we burn piles of dead horses and mules.
The fumes of burning and putrid flesh
are almost unbearable,
and it takes forever to reduce those piles to ash.

UNION SOLDIER.
Two of us rambled out onto the field.
The first dead rebel I came upon
was lying on his back,
his face in agony.
I took a button from his coat as a souvenir.
Some fell with musket gripped so tight
that musket and hands could scarcely be separated.
There were places where the dead lay so close,
I think one could walk two acres and not step off bodies.

UNION SOLDIER.
I passed the corpse of a beautiful boy in gray.
He was about my age,
blond curls scattered about his face,
hands folded peacefully across his breast.
He was clad in a bright and neat uniform,
nicely trimmed with gold,
which told the story of a loving mother and sisters
who'd sent their darling boy to the field of war.
At the sight of that boy, I burst into tears,
and moved on.

UNION SOLDIER.
(*Singing* "The Vacant Chair." *A spotlight shines on a vacant chair*).

> We shall meet, but we shall miss him.
> There will be one vacant chair.
> We shall linger to caress him,
> while we breathe our evening prayer.
> When a year ago we gathered,
> joy was in his mild blue eye.
> But a golden cord is severed,
> and our hopes in ruin lie.
>
> We shall meet, but we shall miss him.
> There will be one vacant chair.
> We shall linger to caress him,
> when we breathe our evening prayer.

(*The spotlight goes out.*)

UNION SOLDIER.
Here beside a great oak tree,
I counted the corpses of fifteen men,
laying about as if, during the night,
suffering from their wounds,
they crawled together for mutual support.
Blue and gray mingled together! What a peculiar sight!
And yet, I observed all over the field,
bodies of Federals and Confederates lying side by side,
trying to console each other as they died.

Here and there in the mud stood wounded horses,
heads drooping, eyes glassy and gummy,
waiting patiently for the slow coming of death.

THE FIGHT AT "FALLEN TIMBERS," THE LAST SKIRMISH

COMMENTATOR.
On Tuesday, April 8,
Sherman led a mixed brigade
to determine whether all Confederates
were in retreat.
On a ridge called "Fallen Timbers"—
that place was littered with dead trees—
Sherman encountered a Confederate cavalry
of about three hundred men
commanded by Colonel Nathan Bedford Forrest.

Forrest's assignment had been
to alert the retreating Confederates
of any pursuit by the Federals
and to defend the Confederate field hospital nearby.

Sherman's men, outnumbering Forrest's,
charged up the hill,
while Forrest and his men charged down,
screaming like wild men.
Forrest, far in the lead of his troops,
fired right and left with his pistols,
frightening Sherman and his staff
into fleeing to safety and taking cover
behind his own brigade,
whereupon Forrest ran out of ammunition.
A Federal shot him in the hip,
and Forrest and his men
retreated into the woods.

Sherman's admiration for Forrest's bold charge
was unbounded, and he later wrote
if Forrest had not run out of ammunition,
"my career would have ended right there."

The fight at Fallen Timbers was the final skirmish.
The battle of Shiloh was now completely over.

NEAR THE PEACH ORCHARD

UNION SOLDIER.
During the first day's fighting,
wide tracts of woodland caught fire,
and scores of wounded who might have recovered
perished by slow torture.
We found several hundred bushels of corn with husks
all in a pile.
Many wounded soldiers crawled there
apparently to make themselves more comfortable.
When fire swept through the woods and over the corn,
those poor men couldn't escape.
Most were in postures of agony,
which spoke of the torment of the flame.
Clothing was half-burnt away, hair and beard completely.
The contraction of muscles turned hands to claws,
and gave faces a hideous grin.
The rain had come too late.

UNION SOLDIER.
Bodies lay half buried in the ash, some relaxed,
denoting a merciful bullet's bringing them sudden death.

COMMENTATOR.
Did a kind companion kill them off one by one
and then kill himself?

UNION SOLDIER.
Down in a ravine sits our Company bugler,
leaning against a tree. His form is rigid.
His last moment came
while reading a letter still held in his hand.
His bugle had been cut away from the cord around his neck.

UNION SOLDIER. (*Singing* "The Minstrel Boy").

> The Minstrel Boy to the war is gone;
> in the ranks of death you will find him.
> His father's sword he hath girded on,
> and his wild harp slung behind him.
> "Land of Song!" said the warrior-bard,
> "tho' all the world betrays thee.
> One sword at least thy rights shall guard,
> one faithful harp shall praise thee."

UNION SOLDIER.
I saw a Union soldier,
his mouth so crammed with cartridges his cheeks bulged,
and bullets protruded from his mouth.
Rebels did this.

UNION SOLDIER.
I took from the body
of a fine looking, gray haired Confederate
a beautifully written letter
dated at Memphis a few days before.

It was from his daughter,
lamenting his absence in the most tender terms,
and giving thanks to God that in just a few short days
his term of enlistment was coming to an end,
and he'd be returning home,
never to leave his family again.

UNION SOLDIER.
One dead Confederate officer was covered
with a makeshift housing of rails.
On it was a leaf torn from a notebook
with the following penciled words:
"Federals, respect my father's corpse!"

Many of our boys wanted to cut off
the beautiful buttons and gold cord,
but our Colonel had the body guarded
as if it belonged to a saint.

UNION SOLDIER.
I rode over to the Hornets' Nest.
In the tangled brush
lay the headless, the trunkless, the disemboweled.
Others were completely intact and still alive
but not complaining,
walking about in a dazed and helpless state,
mutely appealing for the help that none could give.

UNION SOLDIER.
I entered my father's camp.
I heard my father'd been killed,
and his regiment had gone in pursuit of rebels.
Every tent had been pillaged.

The rebels had exchanged dirty blankets for clean ones,
and left worn out brogans for new boots and shoes.
They'd taken all the food.
Everywhere were signs of feasting and revelry
during their one night of glorious victory.

Later that evening my father's regiment returned,
with none other than my father riding at the head!
When he saw me, he dismounted,
took me in his arms,
and gave me the most affectionate embrace
I can ever remember.
For the first time in my life,
I knew my father loved me.

UNION SOLDIER.
The smoke had cleared, and the sun shone brightly.
The green clad trees cast a cooling shade.
But a deathlike silence brooded over us.
We did not see a living creature—
except buzzards and carrion crows—
no squirrels, no birds,
and we did not hear a cricket's chirp
to disturb the suffocating silence.

The dead of both armies lay thick—
some bloated so
that the buttons popped off their waistbands,
others with bloody froth oozing from their mouths,
flies buzzing about like bees.
And all around, filling the air, a putrid smell.

UNION SOLDIER.
North of a peach orchard,
a poor Federal lies in a broken down ambulance—
the team killed, the driver covered with blood and dirt,
both legs and an arm shot nearly off.
He keeps saying,
"Where is my regiment? I want my regiment!
When are they coming back for me?"

Was it an oversight he was left behind? Perhaps.
Can he survive? Maybe.
Will he survive? Doubtful.

UNION SOLDIER.
Arriving at the Hornets' Nest, what do I find?
Our adjutant alive and sitting all alone.
See him pull at his eye!
He received a bayonet thrust in his temple,
which caused the eye to leap out of its socket;
he has pulled at it till the optic nerve
is out at full length. How it pops
when the eyeball slips out of his hand!

UNION SOLDIER.
The face of the earth is torn
and spattered with blood.
Sorrow prevails, and no one talks.
Everyone seems asleep,
the living and the dead,
resting together.

UNION SURGEON.
All the wounded are brought to the Landing.
Making no preparations for battle here—
let alone one of such magnitude—
created a great deal of unnecessary suffering.
You know very well which of our generals
must be blamed for that.

The want of adequate care
gave me the keenest agony I've ever endured.
Many perished for want of water and food.

I have to say that there were a few dedicated surgeons
who did what they could,
but they were young and inexperienced.

Then there were the adventurer-surgeons,
because of whose reckless cutting and carving,
many men perished.

And then there were the wanton-surgeons,
who, instead of caring for the suffering,
completely abandoned them,
and spent their time riding horses for amusement
or seeking trophies in the fields.

Even among the dedicated,
most would look on for awhile
or dress two or three of the slightly wounded,
then suddenly leave.

I had to do all the major operations myself,
assisted by a hospital steward and two nurses.

But the number of the wounded
required an army of surgeons.

UNION SOLDIER.
Gangrene had set in
in a badly shattered arm.
I stood by the table
and applied cool compresses to his forehead
and gave him brandy to drink
and ether to breathe
until he was unconscious.
Three doctors then began their work.

UNION VOLUNTEER NURSE.
Many soldiers were men in their fifties,
and many were boys in their teens.

UNION DOCTOR.
I practiced medicine for ten years,
but I knew nothing about surgery,
except what I'd read in textbooks.
We found ourselves destitute
of everything necessary to do our job.

I filled out a requisition, and gave it to three men
to deliver to the hospital supply boat.
The requisition was returned, explaining
that papers "not going through channels"
could not be recognized.

I wrote a complaint to General Grant,
and I delivered it to him myself at the Landing.
I saluted him, then handed it to him.

He could tell by my dress that I wasn't an orderly.
Even so, he didn't even bother
to look at the requisition,
and turning somewhat away, he said,
"Papers not going through channels
are not recognized here!"
By the time he finished his sentence,
he'd completely turned his back on me.

I left, totally flattened,
feeling as if he'd dumped
a barrel of ice water on me.
If I held any admiration for Grant up to that moment,
let me simply say,
after that, I admired him less.

Our quartermaster sent out a detail
to bring in the cows and calves
turned out by the fleeing inhabitants.
The calves were killed, and Mrs. Johnson, our cook
combined the veal and milk with rice
working them into an elegant stew.

That diet improved our patients
more than any drugs they'd received.

UNION SOLDIER.
Many wounded were shipped to hospitals up north.
The slightly wounded were ferried to Savannah, Tennessee.
Some were placed in tents,
and these recovered more quickly than those in houses.

UNION SOLDIER.
General Will Wallace was taken to the Cherry home,
where General Grant made headquarters
before deciding to come to Pittsburg Landing.
General Wallace did not know where he was,
and Mrs. Wallace was the only person he recognized.
He showed his delight at her presence
by patting her on the waist and squeezing her hand.
Most of the time, he dropped into a stupor,
and whenever he came to,
he'd pass his fingers over every hand
until he touched her ring.
At last he pressed her hand to his heart,
and said, "We meet in heaven,"
and passed away.

UNION SOLDIER.
At the Landing the dead are so numerous
trenches are cut in a field.
Rebels are buried first, Union last
to afford their family an opportunity to identify them.

The mounds had rough headboards planted over them,
made from the sides of a cracker box
or a cracker barrel stave,
while sometimes a pen of rails was built around a grave.

Little red or yellow mounds rise rapidly in the woods.
They are marked, but the markings won't last,
and the identity of the men will soon be lost.

The burial party dug a trench about fifty feet long,
six feet wide, and three or four deep.
The rebel dead were brought there all afternoon.

I saw more than twenty bodies on the side of the trench.
The bodies were laid side by side on their backs
in the bottom of the trench, and the earth shoveled in.
A little heap of yellow clay marked their sepulcher.

UNION SOLDIER.
Burial details gathered up the bodies
and placed them in wagons,
hauling them next to the trench,
piling them up like cord wood.

UNION SOLDIER.
We were given plenty of whiskey,
and I firmly believe
we couldn't have done the job without it.

A hundred eighty corpses were thrown into a gully.
The burial detail climbed on top,
straightening out the arms and legs,
tramping them down
to make the pit hold as many as possible.

In places the earth was so soggy
the shallow pits we dug promptly filled with water.
Corpses were tossed in
and landed with a splash
and then a bump when they hit bottom.

Some of our men kicked the Secesh into those pits.
One fell on his face with a thud.
The more humane among us tried to roll him over.

"Oh, leave him face down,"
sassed a Union man from Missouri,
"for when he scratches,
he'll be heading in the right direction!"

UNION SOLDIER.
By the time we buried the last of the dead,
a green mold had overspread their features,
making them even more ghastly.
It was nighttime when we finished our task.

Lots of citizens come every day
to dig up their dead and take them home.
It would be better to leave them where they are.

COMMENTATOR.
When Beauregard asked Grant to call a temporary truce
so the Confederates could bury their dead,
Grant harshly said, no truce was necessary
for the burial of the Confederate dead
"is already accomplished."

During and after the Confederate retreat,
Beauregard maintained that the battle of Shiloh
was a great victory for the South,
and that his retreat was, in his words,
his "most brilliant and successful" strategy
for the South to achieve that victory.
This incredible nonsense brought him nothing but ridicule.
Nonetheless, Beauregard maintained this fantasy
until his dying day.

EPILOGUE

UNION SOLDIER.
General Grant was under a cloud
because of the surprise attack at Shiloh,
which came so near to defeating us.
It was a common sight to see him riding about
and receiving little attention from the other generals.
Even so, most of the men in the ranks had confidence in him.
His plain and unassuming manner
made him a great favorite with the volunteers,
who had no love of the regulars.

Some of our great generals deny
that Shiloh was a surprise.
But no one, however exalted, has the right to deny the truth.

COMMENTATOR.
The truth is, there was a great failure in leadership,
North and South, at Shiloh,
which resulted in the extraordinary carnage
in a battle that lasted only two days:

Union casualties:
1,754 killed,
8,408 wounded,
2,885 missing.
Total: 13,047.

Confederate casualties:
1,728 dead,
8,012 wounded,
959 missing.
Total: 10,699.

American casualties:
Total: 23,746.

UNION MARCHING BAND (*Playing*) and UNION
CHORUS (*Singing* "The Battle Hymn of the Republic").

> Mine eyes have seen the glory
> of the coming of the Lord.
> He is trampling out the vintage
> where the grapes of wrath are stored.
> He hath loosed the fateful lightning
> of his terrible swift sword.
> His truth is marching on.
>
> Glory, glory, hallelujah!
> Glory, glory, hallelujah!
> Glory, glory, hallelujah!
> His truth is marching on.

THE END

ABOUT THE AUTHOR

Howard Rubenstein is a physician, writer, and photographer. He was born in 1931 in Chicago, where he graduated from Lake View High School. He received a B.A. from Carleton College, where he was elected to Phi Beta Kappa and Sigma Xi and won the Noyes Prize for excellence in ancient Greek. In 1957 Rubenstein received an M.D. from Harvard Medical School. In 1967 he was appointed Physician and Chief of Allergy at the Harvard University Health Services. In 1989 he was appointed a Medical Consultant to the Department of Social Services, state of California. In 2000 he retired from the practice of medicine.

Howard Rubenstein's translation of Aeschylus' *Agamemnon* was produced by the Granite Hills Acting Workshop, San Diego, in 1997. P.E. Easterling, Regius Professor of Greek, University of Cambridge, England, gave the translation a glowing review, calling it "lively . . . vigorous . . . [with] great directness . . . accessible to modern audiences." Oliver Taplin, Regius Professor of Greek, University of Oxford, called the translation, "vivid and immediate." A videotape of the production may be found in the Archive of Performances of Greek and Roman Drama, Oxford.

Rubenstein's adaptation of Euripides' *The Trojan Women* was produced in San Diego in 2001 and was the "most decorated" show (*San Diego Playbill*) of the 2000-2001 San Diego theater season.

Howard Rubenstein (book and lyrics), in collaboration with Max Lee (music), adapted the thirteenth century Chinese comedy *Xi Xiang Ji* into *Romance of the Western Chamber–a Musical*, which had its world premiere at the Dongpo Theatre, Hangzhou, China, 2011, in Rubenstein's English and with Mandarin supertitles. The Confucius Institute of San Diego State University and its managing director, Dr. Lilly Cheng, won the Asian Heritage Award in Performing Arts, for the year 2011, for promoting bridges between Asian and Western culture and specifically for promoting the Hangzhou production of Rubenstein and Lee's *Romance of the Western Chamber.*

Shiloh is Howard Rubenstein's first narrative play.